Table of Contents

How to Trade Options the Complete Guide for Beginners

Alan Newton

Introduction

In January 2021, a trader in Washington state sold options worth $200,000 on GameStop. He couldn't have predicted that on January 28th GameStop would more than double in value. When that happened, he had to buy back his position at more than $200,000. The trader lost a lot of money and later he would sue Keith Gill, of the GameStop frenzy, for fraud—claiming that Gill was misrepresenting himself as an amateur trader so that he could pump the stock to benefit himself. This is a big deal because options derive their value from an underlying assets like stocks. In this case, it was GameStop.

The first instinct that many traders have when they hear the story is to say that this trade was, for lack of a better word, stupid. It is unusual to put a large amount of money in one trade like this, especially when you are an amateur trader. That is true but that is not why I am telling you the story. I am telling it because it illustrates how risky options trading can be. It can lead to complete losses with nothing to salvage afterward.

It's an example of what can happen if you go into options trading, thinking it's going to be easy and cheap. The fact is that derivatives are complicated, and options are derivatives, so options are complicated too. If you don't know what any of that means, don't worry, we will discuss it later. When faced with that, how can you ensure you are going to make the right decisions when trading options? That your approach is appropriate and effective? You can assure yourself by learning specific things, building from a well-rounded foundation.

I know that it can be done. Almost anybody can learn how to trade options despite how difficult they are. I know this because I've taught myself. I've studied markets, stocks, and options trading and I have been successful at it. What you are about to learn from me has given me financial freedom and time to spend with my family. With the popularity of trading, there has been an explosion of material online, from all kinds of people, purporting to teach beginners how to trade options. Most of this material is either not written for beginners in mind, is sparse, or does not share best practices and tools. What good is knowledge if you don't know how to apply it? This is why I wrote this book. This book is educational in nature, but teaches habits, tricks, and other practical skills that will help you. Here's what you will learn.

We will begin our journey with an outline of options. We will talk about options at their most fundamental and how they function. At this point, we will not get into the details of the kinds of options that are out there and how they function. The point of the first chapter is just to situate you with the idea of options which will be the knowledge that all the other chapters will build upon.

In the second chapter, I will go into the details of options. We will discuss the terms and definitions that are related to options and the basic types of options. We'll talk about where options are listed and how the buying and selling of options works. Then we will turn to factors that affect options prices. Next, we discuss trading habits and common mistakes that beginners make. At this point, you will begin to see a more well-rounded picture of options trading begin to fall.

In the third chapter, we talk about the practicalities of options trading, like how you set up your account, choosing your broker, and what that has to do with your budget and risk tolerance. Then we will discuss how to spot trading opportunities and how to formulate a trading plan.

In the fourth chapter, you're going to learn about how to choose the right assets and options. It's no good learning all this information without learning how to pick winners. You will learn about aspects of an asset you need to look at to predict what direction the asset will move. In options trading, this is very important.

Chapter five is all about strategies. We talk about beginner-friendly strategies in what circumstances the strategies work. We show how they function and what are common investor theses that accompanies them.

Then you will learn what to assess the risks and rewards associated with them. Once you've done that, you will learn how to choose the right strategy for your goals. It would be boring if we just stopped there. In the end, we introduce you to more intermediate strategies that offer both safe and secure gains.

In chapter six, we'll see that options trading is one of the most diverse financial instruments that support a wide range of expertise and comfortability. Anyone with confidence in a particular asset can find an option that will work for them. So, you aren't limited to stock options, which are the most popular kind of options out there.

In the seventh chapter, we discuss the emergence of meme stocks and what that means for options trading, and how they can be approached. It's more of an open discussion of the issues than a lesson.

Finally, in the last chapter, we'll talk about various ways that you can monitor your trades and a few tips to improve your skills as a trader.

I enjoyed writing this book and I know you will learn a lot from it. I hope you are excited about it as I am.

Chapter 1: Overview of Options Trading

This chapter is an overview of options. It is to give you an idea of what to expect as we move forward. Think of it as a way of situating your expectations and preparing you for what's ahead.

Without wasting any time, let's begin with the obvious question.

What Are Options?

At a fundamental level, options are contracts that allow the people who hold them the right to buy or sell a financial asset. A financial asset may be stocks, bonds, ETFs, futures, or others. There's a wide variety of options out there and each contract will have a negotiated price, which is the agreed-upon price that the financial asset will be sold or bought. They also have an expiry date, which is the last date when the negotiated price is valid.

The option holder merely has the right to buy the underlying financial asset at a predetermined price before the expiry date. The option holder isn't required to do anything, whether to buy or sell the underlying financial asset before the expiration date. It's up to them if they want to do that. It's important to understand that the contract doesn't bind you to do anything, it only gives you an option to buy or sell an underlying security or financial asset. Maybe that is why they're called options. Options are considered derivatives in financial markets because they derive their value from the value of an underlying asset;

when we are talking about stock options, that means the option derives its value from stock or its underlying asset.

Trading options is the act of buying and selling options contracts on financial markets. Options can be traded or speculated much the same way as you do with stocks, bonds, and other financial assets. But buying a stock options contract is different from actually having invested in company stock. When you buy a stock options contract, you've merely bought the privilege to buy the stock at a predetermined price before the expiry date, but you do not actually own the stock.

This is different from trading stocks themselves. For one example, when you buy stocks, whether you are speculating them or not, you have essentially owned the shares of that company, so you have become an investor no matter how temporary that status is. The same thing doesn't happen with stock options. As I've said, that is because when you buy an option you have merely bought a right to buy or sell the underlying asset as a specific price is before the expiry date.

Owning an options contract allows you to do three things with them. The first one is to buy or sell shares of an underlying company or some asset. Second, you can sell the same options contract to somebody else who is interested. Thirdly, you can walk away from the option without having exercised it or sold it and allow it to expire.

Options contracts allow you to speak to speculate on whether an asset price is going to rise or fall. They also allow you to speculate by how much the price of the underlying asset is going to rise and fall, and in the timeframe that the change will occur. Your chances of making a profit relying on being able to predict those elements of an underlying asset.

An optional contract will allow you to profit from your position in one of the following ways. You can sell that options contract at a higher price than you bought it for, or you can sell or buy the underlying asset at a higher/lower price than it is going for, allowing you to profit from the difference.

With the popularization of trading and the gamification of trading and investing, there's been a lot of information going around from purported experts that can be confusing for beginners. Some of it is flawless and some of it is misguided and actually dangerous. In this section, we are going to look at some of the most popular misconceptions concerning options. At this moment, options are one of the most popular financial instruments. For instance, they were very instrumental in the GameStop frenzy that we saw on January 28th this year. This makes it very important to set the record straight.

Now, without wasting any time, let's get into it.

One: It's Very Easy to Make Money With Options

At first it might appear that it is easy to make money with options trading, but options trading is one of the most difficult ways to make money on markets. It has a long, steep learning curve, and you will realize, as you trade options, that you never stop learning. There's always something new to learn. There is always some new way to look at things and re-evaluate. So, the idea that options trading is very easy and you can do it without any preparation is just misguided.

You should expect that it's going to take a very long time to get into it and that there'll be a lot of factors to consider when your options trade. That means you often must get a host of things right, and the complicated nature of options, which will become apparent, doesn't make things any easier.

Lastly, as evidence, if options trading was that easy, everybody would just do it and they would be successful at it. We would all be encouraging each other to drop everything and trade options because options are the route to financial independence.

Two: Options Are a Zero-Sum Game

When you put it like that it sounds very risky and therefore very highly rewarding, but they aren't an all-or-nothing game. Both sellers and buyers can make a profit on the same options contract if they've played it right.

There's no reason to assume the amount of profit you make from an options contract is proportional to the loss. That depends on the option seller. It might occur that they have employed strategies that have allowed them to absorb that loss and they expected it. It's possible for them to make an even larger profit than the one that you have made from the trade. This will become more apparent in later chapters.

Three: Options Are Too Risky

Options, like other kinds of derivatives, are often thought to be too risky. This is another mischaracterization of options. Options are only risky if you have no idea what they're doing.

The lack of understanding might lead you to get into where you stand to potentially lose a lot of money.

However, options strategies come in different shapes and sizes. There are more conservative ones, which limit and control risk. Then there are more risky ones, but you find that most of the popular options strategies are safe.

Also, options allow you to know in advance the maximum you will lose on a trade. That means you can avoid losing more money than you had planned, making it one of the safest ways to invest, especially if you don't have a lot of money.

Four: Options Are Short Term

Another ongoing misconception is that options are short-term, but options come in various sizes.

For instance, there are options that last a week, a month, a quarter, and even years.

LEAPs stand for long-term equity anticipation securities, and they are the longest options, expiring after three years. So, there's something for anybody, whether you're a more long-term minded or short-term focused person.

Five: You Need a Lot of Luck to Trade Options

Options trading isn't like a slot machine. You need to approach it like it's a business with a business plan and a smart strategy. Do not think about it as making bets that might turn out your way. A few small wins achieved at lower risk will work better than one big risky play that gives you a win.

What's important when it comes to options trading is not going for the occasional 500% win but having a trading plan that's consistent and safe.

That gives you returns on a regular basis. What matters is the overall picture, not how much you make on each trade.

Six: You Can Fail on a Lot of Trades and Win on That Big One

Another misconception that we hear a lot is that you can fail on a lot of trades and have a few big winners which will make up for all the money that you have lost so far. The problem with that is that you do not know your winning ratio in advance.

For instance, you might have 550% losses before you have a 500% win. If you allocated 10% to each trade on your account, you just had a 50% reduction before you had a chance to enjoy that 500% win.

Seven: Selling Options Is Nearly Risk-Free and Only Sellers Make Money

While it is true that option sellers can win most of the time, it is also true that some losses can be devastating, especially when the seller is inexperienced.

Sellers can make money. But it doesn't make much sense for sellers alone to make money because no one would buy options if they were rigged. For option sellers to attract any business, there must be a real chance that option buyers can also win, or else the business wouldn't work. So there must be a fair chance.

Advantages of Options

The one advantage of options is that they require a smaller initial outlay instead of buying the stock directly. You pay a small amount of money to get the choice to buy or sell the stock at a much later date at what you hope will be below or above market price. And if it does not go well for you have the right to walk away.

Secondly, you can use options to hedge downside risk. You only lose the premium you paid when you bought the options contract. This is better than selling or closing a position prematurely.

Options also offer flexibility for traders.

You can exercise the call option to buy their stocks and add them to your portfolio. You can exercise the call option to buy the shares and then sell all of them, or some of them. Or you can sell your options contracts to another investor when they are in-the-money (more on this later). Or sell an out-of-my-money option to another investor before it expires. A lot of this will begin to make sense when we explain further on options. This is just to give you a taste.

Options give you the ability to fix a stock price on a stock you want to buy in the future regardless of market value at the time. Maybe you're waiting for one of your positions to close so that you have enough capital to enter that stock.

Another advantage is the potential for high returns. You spend less money but potentially make a lot more profit. Options give you more time on a position. You don't have to rush or do anything out of panic. And lastly, options are one of the most strategically versatile financial instruments out there. There are so many ways to use options, allowing you to profit from volatile markets. They're one of the most elegant financial instruments. If you understand them, there's little to stop you from finding creative solutions in difficult financial situations.

Disadvantages of Options

One of the most obvious striking features of options is that they can expire worthless and you would lose the money that you paid for that option. That's one of the most obvious downsides.

Secondly, options can expose an investor to unlimited losses. When an investor writes a put option, he or she is obliged to sell the specified number of shares within the contract period when the option buyer requests. If they don't own those shares, they must buy them on the market and then sell them to the option holder at a loss. Even when the price of those shares is unfavorably high. Since there's no cap on how high a stock price can go, they can lose a lot of money.

Thirdly, stocks require predicting short-term price movements. There's limited time for investing so that requires being able to make two assumptions correctly: the right time to buy the options and when to exercise the options contract.

Some trading strategies will require investors to set up a margin account, which is essentially a line of credit. You will need to put up collateral in case the trade goes against you. Interest rates on margin can range from low single digits to low double-digit. Those costs can run up your trading costs.

Another disadvantage is that there are some options strategies that work well when you run multiple trades at the same time. They can run up your costs a bit.

Options markets aren't as liquid as the stock market. This means trades don't always work perfectly and won't work the way that you intended or hoped. That can be a little daunting and difficult for some people.

Also, options have a steep learning curve compared to stocks. To decide whether to buy stock for the long term, you should know the company's business, its fundamentals, and the environmental and industrial sectors that may impact the success or failure of that business.

You should also be familiar with risks that may impact the stock, but with options, investors need to be hyper-aware of these things and many other things. That's one of the many reasons that trading options is one of the most difficult things to do.

But we're here to learn, and hopefully, when you walk away from this book, you'll have a much clearer idea of what you can expect and how to navigate options trading.

Chapter 2: Trading Fundamentals

In this chapter, we are going to look at how options trading works and some of the logic behind it. Before we go any further, we are going to start by looking at some option trading definitions we will be using in the chapter. It's a good idea that we are clear about what these terms mean, so there's no confusion.

Definitions

Premium: Premium is the price that you pay to buy an options contract.

Strike price: Strike price is a pre-negotiated price you will buy or sell the underlying security according to the options contract. of the security (Yochim, 2016).

Expiration: The date the contract ends where you no longer have the ability to buy or sell at a strike price. In other words, it is the time when you cannot exercise the options contract (Yochim, 2016).

Long: Long implies ownership of something. When you've purchased an option or a stock, you're considered long in that position.

Short: Short means you've sold an option or a stock without actually owning it (Yochim, 2016).

Bid: The price the buyer is willing to pay for an option or any other financial assets selling on the market. If you're selling an option, the bid is the premium you would receive for the contract (Yochim, 2016).

Ask: The price a seller is willing to accept for an option. If you want to buy an option, this is the premium you would pay (Yochim, 2016).

Last: The price that was paid or received the last time the option was traded (Yochim, 2016).

Change: The price change since the previous trading day's low, also expressed in percentage terms.

Volume: The number of contracts traded that day.

Open interest: The number of options contracts currently in play (Yochim, 2016).

In the money: When the strike price is above the price that the stock price for call options. When the strike price is above the stock price for put options.

Exercising an option: When the owner of a call option buys or when the owner of a put option sells the underlying stock at the strike price (Yochim, 2016).

Naked option: An option sold without any previously set aside cash or shares to fulfill the option's obligation. To take profit you would buy the option at a more favorable price, close out the trade and make money on the price differential (Milton, 2021). The strategy has theoretically unlimited downside and is best used by seasoned traders.

Two Types of Options

There are two main types of options out there, call options and put options. In this section, we are going to look at both and explain them and further.

Call Options

A call is an option to buy an underlying asset at a strike price before the expiry date. A call option gives you the right to buy the shares or another underlying asset at the strike price. Having a call option obligates the owner of those shares, who is the person who sold you the option, to sell those shares to you at the strike price.

Call options are profitable if you are expecting the value of the stock to go up because it means you buy the stock at a bargain or under the current market value. Then, as we have talked about, either you can sell the contract for a profit, or you can buy the shares and sell them immediately for a profit. Or you can buy the shares at the bargain and hold on to them.

An example will better explain this. Imagine you have a coupon from a bicycle shop that allows you to buy a bike for $100 that expires in a year. It's up to you when you're going to use that. So, let's imagine that one day the price of a bicycle in the bicycle shop is about $50. You would not find it useful to use the coupon because you would have to spend $100 when you can get it for half that price.

If suddenly the price of the bike is about $200, then the coupon will have a value of over $100, because it means you'll be able to get a bike for $100. So, the coupon is worth using when the price of a bike is above $100. In this case, it has a value of $100. It's up to you when you're going to use it, and it's much more useful if you use it when it's profitable to you.

As long as the price is below $100 it makes sense to hold onto it and not use it. You are hoping that in a year the price of a bike will go beyond $100, and the coupon would be worth using. There is a possibility that this may never happen. That the coupon might expire worthlessly.

That's how call options work. They're like coupons to buy a stock at a specific price. Now let's see how this example functions in the stock market. If you buy a call option from Apple which is currently selling at $120.00 per share with a strike price of $130.00 per share and will expire in a month. That means in a month you'll have the right to buy 100 shares of Apple at $130 per share. That would be you exercising your call option and the call option writer will be obliged to sell you 100 shares at $130 when you exercise your call option. Because the current price of Apple is $120, it is not a good idea to exercise your options contract because it would mean you buy 100 shares of Apple at $130 per share when you can easily get them for $120.00 per share.

So, you wait. If during this time the price of Apple goes up to $250 it is profitable for you to exercise your call option. Option writer will be obliged to sell you a hundred Apple shares at $130. If you want. You would then sell them immediately and make a profit for $250 per share when you got them at a bargain. That is a difference of $120. If you paid $10 per share for the options contracts, you would have made a profit of $110 per share. That is a total profit of $11000 ($110 x 100) when your initial investment was $1000 ($10 x $100).

Now it is possible for the call option to expire worthless, which means to expire without the potential of it making you any profit. That happens when the price of the stock does not rise high enough to warrant exercising the call option; just like in a bicycle coupon example, you didn't find it valuable to use it while the price of bicycles was well below what your coupon was worth. The same thing applies. When an option expires worthless you lose the premium you paid to get it.

Put Options

Put options are the opposite of call options, "[t]hey give you the right to sell shares at a strike price before the expiration date" (Johnson & Lewis, 2010). They are often used to protect positions in a down risk. When you exercise the put option the put writer will be obliged to buy 100 shares from you at the strike price. Put options are good when you think prices will go down because they give you the right to sell your stock or another asset above market value. Exercising a put option is deemed valuable when the price of the underlying asset falls below the striker price.

Now, here's an example. Imagine you own a house worth $1,000,000. You have been intending to sell it so that you can move, and you have a reason to believe that because of some ongoing crisis the price of your house might drop to about $700,000. Now, you have invested a lot in your house, and you don't want to sell it for less than $900,000. In that situation you could buy insurance that allows you to sell your house at $900,000 if it drops in value before the year ends. The insurance will buy the house from you and you would have to pay a premium for that insurance. If you're right and the value of the house drops to about $700,000, you would exercise your insurance and sell the house for $900,000. If you are very cheeky, you could then buy it back at $700,000, its current value, and pocket the $200,000. If you're wrong about the price drop, you would have only spent your premium on the insurance (that money is gone forever), but you will still get to sell your house for $1,000,000.

So that's how put options work, but for stocks and other financial assets. So, if you own 100 shares of Microsoft and you are worried because of recent business performance, the stock price might fall. At the same time, you don't want to close your position yet because there is a chance it might not. So, you buy a put option as a kind of insurance.

Thinking about put options in this way makes it easier to understand them.

Stock options are listed on the New York Stock Exchange. Below is an example of a stock options quote.

NOK AUGUST 24, 2021 PUT AT $1.80

It's worth explaining what each part of the quote means so that you don't get confused the next time you see it. You should understand that stock options quotes may be put together friendly by the trading platform or source that you're using. But it won't be too different from what I'm showing you now.

Starting from the left-hand side, the first thing you encounter is the stock symbol, which is the underlying of the option. In this case, it is the Nokia Corporation. The second item from the left is the expiry date of the options contract. In this case it is August 24th, 2021.

The third item is the type of option. In this instance, it is a put option. Lastly, the last item tells us the premium for the put option. It is $1.80. As you will notice, there's nothing said about the number of shares involved. This is because an options contract typically has 100 underlying shares. So, if you were to buy this put option it would cost you $180 because it's 100 multiplied by $1.80.

Buying and Selling Options

The people who sell or make options are called options writers and the people who buy them are called option holders/buyers. Option holders buy options for the right/choice to sell or buy the underlying stock or the option itself. The amount option holders pay to buy the options is called the premium. The amount that options writers receive is the premium; that is the only profit they hope to make if there is only one option contract.

Depending on how the prediction of the option holder goes, the option holders may exercise the option or sell the option contract to someone else. An option holder can buy and sell puts and buy and sell calls on the market. Options holders have a little risk to worry about because the premium they spend is the maximum that they can lose on a trade. In contrast, the options writers are exposed to much more risk and loss. Depending on how it goes, that may buy back the options contracts they sold to close a position. The option writers are obliged to fulfill their side of the contract if you decide to exercise your options contract. Only about 10% of options are exercised, 30% expire worthless, and about 60% of options buyers make money from buying and selling options instead of the act of exercising options themselves.

What Affects the Price of Options?

In this section, we are going to discuss factors that have an impact on the price of an options contract.

The first one is **intrinsic value**. An option's intrinsic value is the difference between an option's strike price and the underlying asset price. If the call option has a strike price of $30 and the stock price is $35 at present, that means the option has an intrinsic value of $5.

However, a put option will have intrinsic value when the opposite is true. If it happens that the stock price of the put option is lower than the put's, that put option has intrinsic value.

Now options with intrinsic value tend to be a little bit more costly than options that don't have intrinsic value.

The second factor that affects an option's prices is **extrinsic value**, also known as time value. Extrinsic value is about the time until expiry affects an options price. The further away the expiration date is, the more chances that the underlying asset can move into profitability. So, the price of that option tends to be higher, but when the closer the other options contract is to the expiration date, the lower the price because chances of the underlying asset moving into profitability are low.

The third factor is **implied volatility**. Implied volatility is a prediction of the expected volatility of the stock over the period of the options contract. If that stock has high implied volatility that means prices will go up and down more frequently, and the chances of that option contract turning profitable are higher. It means the option will be more expensive. However options with low implied volatility will cost less because chances of them turning profitable are lower.

A lower strike price has more intrinsic value for call options since the option's contract lets you buy the asset at a lower price than what is trading for right now. If the stock price remains, options with intrinsic value will be more expensive. A higher strike price has more intrinsic value for put options because the contracts allow you to sell the stock at a higher price than where it's trading currently. Whenever an option has intrinsic value, it is in-the-money. The at-the-money and in-the-money options tend to be more expensive.

Rules of Trading

This section is all about helping avoid the common pitfalls of trading. If you use this advice, you are much more likely to succeed in your trading.

2% Rule

The 2% rule states that you should only risk 2% of capital on any single trade to limit loss to a small fraction of your accounts. For instance, if you adopt the 2% rule and the risk in your trade is 50%, then you can allocate 4% of your account for that trade. If your risk is only 20%, then you can allocate 10% in a trade. This ensures that if the worst happens, you don't lose all your money. You are forced to diversify your investments because you don't bet on one thing.

Don’t Be Greedy

If you make a 100% profit on a trade, then you should close. It's very rare to make a 100% return so close. Experienced traders learn to get close trades when they've made a profit of about 10%. You're much more likely to be consistent if you close a trade sooner rather than if you stay too long in trade and risk losing all those small gains.

If you're convinced you should stay in position a little longer, then you don't have to abandon the entire position. You can close half of your position and stay. A principle that goes in hand with that is to always play with the house money and always protect your own money.

Understand Time Decay

Make sure that you understand options tend to lose their value with each passing day. This incentivizes getting out of positions in time, instead of waiting too long. Options become completely worthless once they expire, so that's something to think about.

Don't Get Attached

Do not get too attached to a position if you cannot bring yourself to close the position because of some other reason. You should at least initiate a spread strategy. As part of this strategy, you will limit your loss and also limit how much you can make on a trade. We will explore these strategies a little further in detail.

You should also consider selling or purchasing another option with a higher or lower strike price. At least this lets you take some money off the table so that you don't lose everything if the worst happens. It's a bit like what we've talked about in the air about selling half your position.

Practice

Adopt the principle of paper trading your intended strategy and tracking your results, before you put in real money. This is to test your ability to understand what's going on.

Lastly, whenever you get into a position, it doesn't matter which one it is, make a habit of placing limit orders. This will allow you to get some price improvements from the quoted bid or ask price. You don't have to hold onto an option position until expiration. "If your reason for entering a trade changes, then consider exiting the trade to preserve capital" (Peterson, 2017).

Managing Risk

In this section, we're going to look at the ways that we can manage risk. This is one of the most important lessons you could learn.

The first principle is always ensure you are comfortable with the level of risk that you are taking and to never expose yourself to unsustainable losses. In other words, do not put all your savings in a trade or all of your month's salary or anything like that. Whenever you trade or you decide to invest, make sure it's money you're okay with losing because there's always a possibility that you will lose your money. Exposing yourself to extreme risk is highly dangerous and unsustainable. The key to success in trading is consistency and sustainability. So, the moment you get a little too desperate and risk a lot of money, it's not likely to last.

The second one is to always have a backup plan when you enter a trade. Make sure there's a plan. You should know what you are going to do when there's a sudden swing in the stock you are trading. How you're going to exit a trade. How you will cut your losses and conserve capital. You need to consider possible scenarios and plan for them.

Thirdly, evaluate a different payoff scenario. For instance, suppose that you are very bullish on the stock, will it be more profitable for you to buy short, dated options at a lower strike buyer or longer-dated options at a higher strike price? If you are writing a call option what will happen when the option is called as opposed to when it isn't?

The fourth principle is to always follow your trading plan.

After you've initiated your plan, follow it. Your plan is detailed and well-thought-out. It has, ideally, considered all kinds of variables and exit strategies because whenever you enter an options contract you can count the ways it can end. There is no real surprise. So, you should stick to the plan; the plan will tell you when to get out, enter, or stay, if it's a good plan. When a condition for action is met then execute that action. That's what I mean when I say follow the plan. There should be no uncertainty about what those conditions are. State clearly that upon a 2% loss you will do X, and upon 10% profit, you will do Y.

The plan is not a fantasy about how you envision your trade will go. How you wish it would go versus the way things happen are not the same thing, and just because you think something has to happen or will happen, doesn't mean it will.

It sounds ridiculous to say it now, but that is one of the common mistakes that traders make when they trade.

Another principle is to diversify your investments. Diversification means you never invest in just one thing. Consider investing in a multitude of things using different strategies. When it comes to options, you should not put all your money on the same underlying securities. There are different kinds of securities and other options you can trade. It doesn't always have to be stock options. The idea behind diversification is that you aren't reliant on one particular outcome for all your trades to be successful.

Another important habit is to use option orders whenever you enter into a position. For instance, if you use limit orders, you can set the price of when your order can be filled. Thus, you can avoid buying or selling at less favorable prices. There are also other types of orders that help with various aspects of trading like exits. For instance, you can use them to lock in profit or cut losses on a trade. What's neat is that almost all trading platforms will offer you the ability to use orders.

The last piece of advice is to make use of spreads. All options strategies involve the use of spreads. These spreads show us how to manage risk. You can use them to reduce the upfront costs of entering a position and to minimize how much money stands to lose or to gain, potentially reducing the number of things that can go wrong (Sival, 2020). If they sound a little strange right now, we will cover them in detail later.

Common Mistakes That Options Traders Make

Now in this section, we're going to talk about some of these common mistakes options traders make so you can recognize them whenever you see them in others or yourself.

The first one is the antithesis of what we've talked about in the last section; not having a trading plan. So, what's a trading plan? How do you know that you have one?

A trading plan will answer the following questions, and if you find that you can answer these questions, you don't have a trading plan. You're not just trading on feelings.

For instance, a trading plan should tell you how much you are willing to risk on a trade. It should also tell you how you are going to find opportunities in the marketplace, when you're going to enter a position, when and how you are going to exit a position, and how long the trade should take. It should also clarify your goals, the milestones that when reached signify what you should do. Remember, the main advantage of having a trading plan is to take out the feelings in your trade.

The second mistake that traders make is not matching your strategy to outlook. For instance, you might genuinely believe that a stock is not going to perform very well, and you have very good ideas about why it's not going to perform very well within a given week or month. But then you enter a position on the opposite of this idea, or you fail to spot a strategy that can gain from that insight. You might think it's strange, but it happens quite a lot.

The third one is choosing the wrong expiration date. This happens when you don't think about how long your theory or strategy will take to play out. So you underestimate or overestimate the time that it will take for your trading thesis to come to fruition, meaning you lose money. Another thing about expiration dates is that traders falsely assume there will be enough money in circulation to support a trade at the time they close their position. Liquidity is an important factor to consider when it comes to options. Low liquidity means you won't be able to get out of positions as early as you might want, increasing the chances that the contract will expire worthlessly.

Traders also fail to take into account upcoming events and the impact they may have on your positions. For instance, a company's earnings announcement will affect the price movement of stock. So, you should take a look at your calendar and have a pretty good idea of when the best expiration date for your trading thesis will be when you've considered everything. Also, don't sell options with an underlying stock with pending dividends unless you have a high-risk tolerance.

The next mistake is the opposite of what we've talked about in the last section which is choosing the wrong position size. Ultimately when deciding on the trading size, it should be comfortable with the amount of capital you will lose if the trend doesn't go in your favor. Ideally, the trade amount should be large enough to be meaningful, but small enough you don't lose sleep at night.

The next common mistake is ignoring implied volatility. Look at implied volatility whenever you buy an option, it helps you determine the probability the underlying asset will move in your favor. Not only does probability put things into perspective, but it's also essential to understanding the risk-reward ratio of any trading position.

Another mistake is focusing solely on the expiration graph. Solely focusing on the expiration graph doesn't tell you much about the risks a particular option might carry today or in the future.

Another mistake is buying out-of-the-money options. They may be appealing because they're cheap, but they're cheap because they are unlikely to be profitable. If you want to be consistent, you need to focus on the likeliest financial assets.

The next one is using long near-term calls/puts increase for speculation to speculate on the near-term stock movement. Understand that time is working against you, so you will typically need to stock to make a sizable move in a relatively short period of time in order to make a profit.

Many option's option traders prefer to sell near-dated options and take advantage of that accelerated time decay. But as we talked about, liquidity is one of the most important things to look at.

Another mistake is misunderstanding leverage. Most beginners misuse the leverage factor on options contracts and do not realize how much risk they are taking. If you usually trade a hundred shares, then stick to the one option to start. If you normally trade 300 shares, maybe 3 contracts will do. This is a good test of the amount you can start with. If you don't have successes in these sizes, you will most likely not have successes in bigger sizes, so stick to what you can handle.

Another common one is trying to make up for past losses by doubling up. Take small losses so don't ever bet your money with the intent of making it back.

Another common mistake is trading illiquid options. Meaning there isn't enough money to go around, so when you try to get out of a position there is nobody to fulfill your order. A stock that trades more than a million shares a day is liquid. So options trading on that stock will most likely be liquid too.

Another mistake is waiting too long to buy back short strategies. Always be ready and willing to buy back short strategies at an amount that you have initially planned for. If you can keep more than 80% of the initial gain from the sale of an option, consider buying it back immediately (The Options Playbook, n.d.).

Another one is lagging into spreads; most beginners leg into a spread by buying the option fast and selling the second option later. Always treat a spread as a single trade and then try to deal with the workings of timing. You want to get in in the trade before the market starts going down.

Lastly is not being aware of the trade strategies trade-off. Every option strategy has a benefit that corresponds with some tradeoff in exchange for that benefit. Be aware of those parameters.

Chapter 3: How to Start Trading

This chapter focuses on opening an options trading account and other related aspects. Let's get into it.

Opening an options trading account is a little bit more complicated than opening a stock trading account.

To open an options trading account, you need to have a deep understanding of the underlying assets and a host of other things, since options are at the real derivative. Derivatives are, by definition, more complicated.

Opening an Account

"Compared to opening a brokerage account for stock trading, opening an options trading account requires larger amounts of capital" (Royal & Davis, 2021). There are funds to think about, not just about the knowledge required to even begin options trading. Brokerage firms screen potential options traders to assess their trading experience, their understanding of the risks, and their financial readiness.

This is because stock options can get a little bit more complicated, and they can be a lot of balls to juggle. Extra knowledge and perception are required.

It's the brokerage's duty to ensure you are somewhat prepared for what you're getting into. You need to provide the income growth, following investment objectives, capital preservation or speculation, trading experience, your knowledge of investing, how long you've been trading stocks or options, how many trades you make per year, and the size of your trades.

Then will need to provide personal financial information. Your local net worth or investment, annual income, total net worth, and employment information. Then you will disclose investments that can easily be sold for cash. You will also need to specify the types of options you want to trade.

You'll be assigned an initial trading level based on your answers. This is something that most power brokers do. They will give traders a level, which allows them to trade in options with a certain amount of risk or complexity, and as you do better, they will promote you to other levels, which in turn open more features and possibilities.

Choosing a Broker

Look for free resources which could help you with the process such as options trading courses, webinars, one-on-one guidance, or make use of options trading simulations to have a better idea of what your needs might look like. Simulation platforms also help you test your skills before using any real money, so they are very useful too. Brokerages will sometimes offer demo versions of their service, so make sure to use any and explore it. Don't be afraid to test multiple platforms and go with the ones that suit your needs perfectly.

Reliable customer service is also one of the things to look for. A good broker will have reliable customer service that is easy to contact. Because there's money involved, you shouldn't regard a brokerage that is difficult to control to contact and takes a while to respond when there's money at stake.

The tools brookers offer are also important to examine. They should be useful while being easy to use with a decent execution speed. Look at the mobile version of those tools and also compare the premium with the free version if they offer both. This is if we are talking software, it and features. For instance, a frequently updated feed will be one of the most important things, as well as frequent updates for basic charting to help you pick your entry points and exit points. The ability to analyze the trade's potential risks and rewards is also crucial. Examine their screening tools, which will help you filter out assets using a variety of parameters and characteristics. This greatly reduces the amount of work you spend looking for stocks with a specific set of features.

Commissions will also be another deciding factor. There is a spectrum from commission-free alternatives to very expensive brokerages which charge fees and commission per trade. They all have their own advantages, and no one is significantly better than the other, but the deciding factor will be what you are looking for in a broker and your budget. For instance, will you be better served by choosing a broker that offers a single flat rate to trade, or one that charges no commission but likely offers fewer services?

Here are some of the trading platforms you should consider:

- **E-trade** is very good for beginners and has a good overall experience for trading.

- **Trade Station**. Which is known as the trading technology leader. It makes trading in options easy to do.

- **LXTM** is another good one.

- **Charles Schwab** is another great platform to use. Features industries and services like the others.

Then there's **Robinhood**, which is very popular. A lot of people use it, but you should remember that this one and platforms like it might lack that kind of in-depth tools and research tools offered by the platforms we mentioned earlier. There are other cheap, commission-free apps like Robinhood that are meant to be commission-free and make trading a lot cheaper and easier. Among them are companies like Firstrade, AllyInvest, WeBull, and M1 Finance. You might even find they are better than Robinhood.

Most brokerages will set a minimum amount you need to have to trade, so it's something you should take into account when choosing a brokerage. Some may ask for nothing while others may like to have a minimum of $200 to $2,000 in your account.

How to Start

As we've talked about before, you need to develop a trading plan of how you intend to operate your options trading business and manage your risk capital and outline your objectives like capital conversion, generating income growth, and speculation. You're going to have to be really thorough, so there isn't a moment of hesitation or doubt about what should be done should be doing objectives.

You will decide how much you're going to invest and have an entry and exit strategy prepared. When it comes to options, it's wise to start small. Because you can always try more aggressive options strategies, start where you have more experience and knowledge of what you should watch out for and what you should do. In the beginning, it's best to focus on assets that you understand well, to start small and not be unnecessarily aggressive. So, if you understand stocks very well, just focus on stocks before you risk more.

How to Find Great Options Opportunities?

You need to look at derived parameters known as the Greeks which look at the relationship between options and their underlying asset. They are used to describe the sensitivity of an option to factors in an underlying asset and more. The most common are Delta, Gamm, Theta, Rho, and Vega. We will look at them later in more detail. They are one of the most telling things about options and their probability to be profitable.

Second, look at strike prices that are at or near the money. These should ideally expire within two or three months. This gives you the biggest bang for your buck without taking on too much risk.

Try to profit from events, to capitalize off events that will likely affect the share of stock. So, if you buy a call option before an expected excellent earnings report, you can anticipate that it will bring up the specific stock price. Since you invested a lower dollar amount, but benefit just as much as holders of the underlying stock, your percentage gain can soar. If you're wrong about a trade, your downside risk is much lower than for investors owning the stock itself.

Look at historical patterns and analyze them. Stocks often form recognizable patterns on their charts. If you can spot a stock that is about to break out of the upside of its historical pattern, you can buy a call to take advantage of its predictable performance (Money Morning Staff, 2019).

When to Buy, Sell, or Exercise an Option?

You don't need to wait for the expiration date of the option contract to take your profit, you can do this much earlier. So, get out whenever it's a liquid and you have realized your profit. If you're already profitable before expiry, you don't have to wait. If you're not profitable and chances are low you will, you can also close early by selling the option to someone else. There's nothing really binding you to do anything by the expiration date.

Planning Individual Trades

The first thing to do is to make a forecast, which is the outlook on the security you have identified. For instance, you believe the price will go down, up, or both within a span of three months. No matter what your outlook on any given security, there is always a strategy you can use to try and profit from your forecast (*How to Plan Individual Options Trades*, n.d.). It's about making a prediction and forming a strategy based on it.

Secondly, set your targets. The main target you should be setting is how much profit you wish to make, because without knowing how much you are expecting to make, it is impossible to gauge whether or not a trade has been successful.

So, your target tells you if you've been successful or if you failed in a trade. So, for instance, if you aim for a 10% profit on a trade and reach that, your trade is successful. Another target might be the length of time in which you expect a certain trade might turn into profit. This can help you with budget control. You don't want your files tied up in any one trade for too long. Lastly, make sure that the strategy you choose fits with your look. We have already talked about this a bit; we will touch on it again in Chapter 5.

Determine position size before you trade. Position sizing isn't just about how much money you're paying at the point of making a trade, but it's also about how much money you're putting at risk. Once you have done that, pinpoint an entry. Depending on the nature of the opportunity, you may need to wait for a certain criterion to be met before actually making the necessary transactions. In some cases, you may have to act immediately. This is why it's a good idea to have some funds deposited with your broker so you can act quickly when required.

You may need to place multiple orders. In that instance, you should know whether you want those orders to be filled simultaneously or use legging to fill them.

Lastly, prepare your exi, whether you plan to let your position run until expiration, or whether you plan to close them early. You should know what and how you are going to exit and what it looks like. If you set targets for a trade then you should also plan for closing a position, since if you make those targets, your goals will have been reached. You can either monitor the market for when those conditions are met, or you can place automatic orders that do it for you once those targets have been met.

Chapter 4: Evaluating Options

Choosing the right stocks for options is going to be the focus of this chapter, including other related considerations.

Choosing the Right Stocks for Options Trading

The first thing to do is some research.

There are different parameters from which you can evaluate a stock or begin your research. I'm going to go through some of the most reliable and popular ways of doing so.

The first thing to research is some market or industry research. What that entails is getting acquainted with the industry. You should know what the competition is like, what are some of the biggest players, and the strengths and weaknesses of the industry compared to others. In other words, perform a SWOT analysis of the entire industry.

Since most options are short-term, you would not have to do a full deep dive, like looking at whether the industry has a high barrier of entry or the threats facing the industry. Stuff like that rarely matters in the short term. So, you need to keep an eye on factors that are affecting that industry presently, how they present themselves in the day-to-day, and how that might look in a month or the period that you intend to stick to your position.

Look back at the stock performance of the company you are interested in. It's important to look back at how the company has performed in the last month, week, year, or whatever amount of time is most appropriate for your purposes. But I think looking at how the company has performed for at least a year is one of the most responsible things you can do even if you are only interested in how the company is going to perform in the next month. That is because a clearer trend starts forming when you stand back.

You could look as far back as the beginning if you wanted to, but for a call options contract a certain period may be more appropriate for you because you are not looking to invest in the company long term. If your intentions were more long-term you would have to look at the data of about five years or more. However, this is not to say there is no value in looking at data that is older than five years if your mission is holding a contract for a month.

The next thing you do is to look at company earnings. Are they going up or are they going down? What service or product are they selling? Remember, companies exist to make a profit, and if a company is profitable it means it's doing its job and investors like companies that are profitable. That will have a positive effect on the stock movement. If the company is not doing well, its stock performance will suffer.

You should also research upcoming events and how they are going to affect company stock.

You need to also look at the management team. Who are they? What are their experiences? Are they a good fit and will they drive the company in the right direction? Are there any questions or doubts about their ability to do so? Visit the company website, listen to a lot of press releases, and read between the lines. Find out what regions the company operates in and factors that could affect it.

So don't just invest, pick a stock because it looks familiar to you. You have to do some research first and go from there.

The second tip is to choose liquid stocks. Look, liquidity is one of the most important things when it comes to trading. The less liquid stock is, the harder it is to buy or sell it. So, you need to look at a stock that has a high trading volume. If the trading volume is low, you shouldn't trade an option contract based on it because it may be difficult for you to exercise your option or sell it when you need to. So, you have to choose stocks that will allow everything to go smoothly.

Investors use technical analysis to study charts and see if there are any trends the stock is following. Past performance does not always predict how a company is going to perform in the future, but it's one of the most useful tools in doing that. It can give you an idea of what kind of a company or an asset you are dealing with. Investors often use this to find a stock's resistance level and support level.

Look for medium or higher-priced stocks because those see a lot of action overall. There's much more money going around, and they tend also to have some volatility. Volatility is a good thing for options trading.

Look at upcoming events to see how they might affect the implied volatility of the stock. This is important because the implied volatility of an option will affect the options price and tell us about the likelihood that the underlying will move. For instance, an Apple event where they announce new products, features, and services might show a rise or fall in Apple stock.

Consider using stock screeners, which will allow you to evaluate hundreds of stocks using a set of metrics or parameters appropriate for your goals, allowing you to pick the right stocks very easily.

Choosing the Right Options

Now you know how to choose the right stocks for your options, you need to learn how to choose the right options. In this section, I'll focus on tips you can use to choose the right option for your strategy.

The first thing that you need to do is find an asset that you wish to trade. It doesn't matter what it is. It can be an ETF, bonds, or stocks. The most comfortable pick for beginners is stock, so I'll personally focus on that.

The second thing you're going to define is your main objective, the main thing you want to achieve with options trading.

Are you bullish or bearish on the underlying asset? Or do you want to hedge? Or are you looking to speculate options on the contract itself? You need to think of all those things and more before you get into any trade. This step is more to inform how you will approach the following steps in this guide.

Then you need to determine the risk and reward payoff of the trade you want to take depending on your risk tolerance. Then decide on a strategy that fits comfortably with what you are most comfortable with, risk-wise.

Then you need to check the volatility of the asset that you're interested in. Since we are talking stocks, check stock volatility.

High volatility tends to translate to higher premiums. High volatility makes an option more attractive because the chances that the shock will move either way is higher. Low volatility translates to cheaper premiums because chances of the stock moving either are very low, so options writers set lower prices to attract buyers.

Identify events that are important to the financial asset integral to your options contract, based on your thesis. It might be something to do with economic data, the Federal Reserve, upcoming announcements, reports, publications, and press coverage or politics. Whatever it is, it needs to be something that's specific to the stock that you were interested in. Identify how relevant they are for your time frame. Anything beyond that time frame, which will be guided by the time until expiration will be irrelevant, for your options contract.

Then based on that information, you will devise a strategy guided by your risk tolerance. If you are a conservative investor, you want to earn income from premiums before companies announce their quarterly earnings. If you're aggressive, you might want to take a long shot if you are convinced that there will be a big decline within six months by buying puts on stock indices.

Then decide your parameters based on this strategy. For example, you will determine the strike price and the expiration date that can go with that will go well with your strategy. You might, for instance, go for a call option that has a long expiration date at the lowest cost possible.

Now let's go through each of these steps in more detail to really illustrate how they would work in real-life situations.

Determine the Asset

The first thing you do is figure out the kind of asset that you would like to trade, or one you're much more comfortable trading. Whether it's ETFs, indices, bonds, or stocks, it will be up to you. In our example, we are going to use stocks because they are the easiest and the most accessible for most traders.

Objective

Let's say you have $2,000 in your account and you're bullish on Intel stock. Right now, Intel is selling at $66 per share.

Your goal, in this instance, is to buy Intel shares at a bargain. You believe in the upcoming two months or more the stock will rise.

Risk/Reward

You are a new investor, so you are not comfortable with placing all the $2,000 on the bet. So, you settle for maybe spending $1,500 on a bet and saving the $500. You are comfortable with the idea that you might lose all that money.

Volatility

The implied volatility of a month-long call option with the strike price of $68 is 30%. The three-month-long call options on the market with the same strike rate has an implied volatility of 20%. Overall, market volatility is 15%.

Events

There's nothing exciting going on with Intel at the moment. It doesn't look like there'll be new announcements anytime soon. Announcements of products and services are expected towards the end of the year. So, in this instance, your bet is informed by other reasons, like you believe the stock is undervalued.

Strategy

Your strategy is simple. You want to buy a cheap out-of-the-money call option at about $1.00 premium with the strike rate of $68.00 per share that expires in three months. An out-of-the-money call option would be cheap and appropriate for longer time periods.

Parameters

You have two options. You have a month long call option, with a strike price of $68 that costs $0.50 per share. Then you have a three-month call option with a strike price of $68 dollars that costs $0.25 per share.

What You Do

Finally, you decide to go for the second three-month call option that costs $0.25 per share but you're only willing to spend $1,500 of your money. If you buy these call options with that money, you will get 60 of them which will have 6,000 shares as their underlying.

If you're wrong and nothing happens in three months, you would have lost the entire $1,500. If you are lucky and Intel announces a big deal with another large tech company, the stock will go up. Let's say it goes up by $10, the stock will now be worth $76 per share.

That means your position would have an intrinsic value of $7.75 per share. This means your position will be worth $46,500. Now, you can sell the option on the market for that price and you would have made a profit of $45,000. Or you can exercise the call option and buy the shares. Then profit off those shares. What you do in the end will be up to you, but you would have followed the steps above to better formulate and execute your strategy.

Trading Strategy

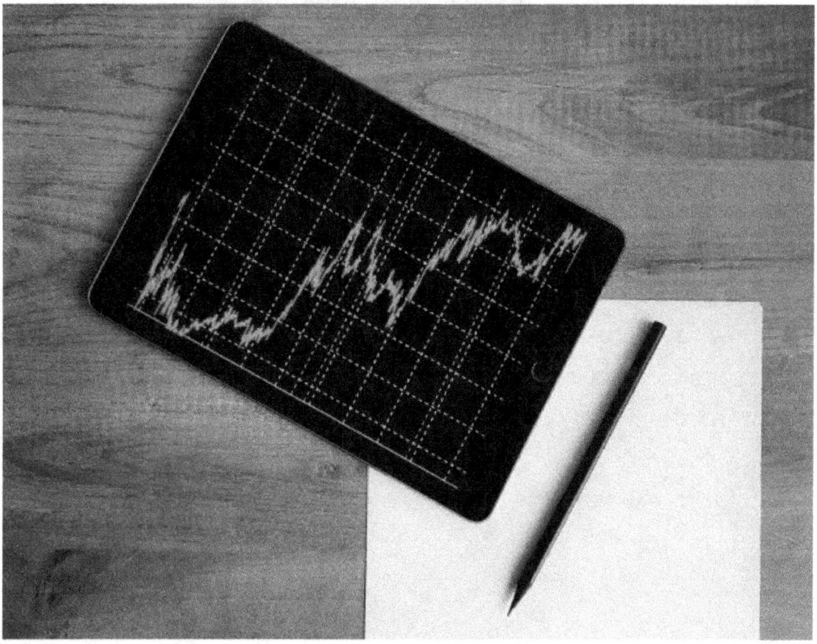

In this section, we'll focus on some of the things that you have to study before you decide on an options strategy. The first thing that you're going to need to do is to decide which direction you think the stock is going to go. If you think the price will rise, that means you'll have to buy a call option. And if you think the price will fall that means you have to go with a put option.

Once you've decided where you think the stock price will go, think about how much you think the price is going to move in either direction. The next step, depending on how much you think the option will move in that direction, is to decide on the strike price (or options contract) that reflects the belief. For example, if the implied volatility of that stock is not very high, you might need to buy both puts and calls on the stock.

Since low implied volatility means the stock may not move in the way that you want, they're cheap to buy. If your bet turns out right it pays for itself because you made so little. Inexpensive bets that may pay big are sometimes called for.

Once you've thought about those details, then you should think about the time you think it will take for your thesis to happen. In other words, the amount of time the option contract needs to be profitable. You should know if you need a weekly option or a monthly option for instance. Shorter expirations tend to work best for experienced traders, while longer expiration is more beginner-friendly because of the chance that the thesis is going to be higher, but they cost more. A longer expiration date also gives you time to sell your options contract if you want.

How Do You Pick the Right Strike Price?

There are few steps that you can follow.

The first one is your risk tolerance. Your risk tolerance should dictate whether you're going to buy an in-the-money option or an out-of-the-money option, or at-the-money option. It should be one of the important determinants of what you're going to do.

For instance, an in-the-money call option means that when the stock price rises, you're likely to make more money than if it was another call option. But these tend to be expensive and if the stock price doesn't rise enough, you would lose a lot of money than if you had paid for an at-the-money or out-of-the-money call options, but then again chances are lower that those would turn profitable. The expiration date will also be another telling factor; the further an option is from it, the higher the chances it will be profitable, but it costs more, and vice versa.

Once you've thought about that, you need to think about the amount of capital you are comfortable with risking. You need to remember that an out-of-the-money call option may yield higher reruns but the chances of that coming to fruition are less when compared to in-the-money options. Therefore, they often cost less.

If you're a conservative investor, you might go for an in-the-money or at-the-money option. If you have high-risk tolerance, you might go for an out-of-the-money option. Regardless of what you choose you need to accept you will lose all your premium if you are wrong.

How to Predict Price Movement

You might wonder how you're supposed to tell where the price of a stock is going to move. What are some of the indicators that you need to look at? In this section, we are going to look at how we can do that.

Pull Call Ratio (PCR)

The first thing that you need to look at is the pull call ratio. This value is calculated by dividing the number of traded put options by the number of traded call options (Murphy, 2021). A pull call ratio of above 1 means that there are more sellers than buyers, meaning that the market is bearish. When it is less than one, then there are more buyers and sellers, meaning that the market is bullish.

It's one of the most common and trusted ratios out there that look at investor sentiment. If sentiment is high, it might imply that the price is going to go up.

But it's worth knowing that historical data from November 26, 2006 to September 2015 shows an increase in the Chicago Board Options Exchange (CBOE) PCR equities-only values were followed by declines in the S&P 500, vice versa.

When using PCR for prediction, you need to pay attention to the PCR value threshold or bands. The PCR value breaking above or below the threshold indicates a market move.

VIX Index

Another important indicator is the VIX index which combines all implied volatility on a diverse set of options based on the S&P 500. The VIX index provides a single number that presents the overall implied volatility in the market. A large VIX movement is often followed by movements in the market in the opposite direction.

Daily Moving Averages

Another thing to look at is daily moving averages. The daily moving average is used to identify the trend of price movement over a period. Now to figure out which direction the price is going to go, you need to be able to predict how much the price is expected to move.

This will require a few steps. The first thing that you have to do is to retrieve an options chart for stock that you are interested in and pick an expiry date in the future. Secondly, look at the option strike prices on the chain. Identify the one which is closest to the current market value of your symbol. Thirdly, add the premium of the first call option and the pulled option of the strike price from the second step. Then, to the value above, add the premium of the first call option strike higher than the one in the second step, and add the premium of the first put option strike lower than the one in the second step.

Divide the new total value by two and just like that, you have the dollar amount the stock price is expected to be over that period. The number only calculates magnitude, and it changes over time, so you need to calculate it a couple of times over several days. You can also change the expiry date to find out what the expected move is for one week, a month, or whatever time period you are most comfortable with.

Technical Analysis

Technical analysis will help us identify entry and exit signals in even markets. "Momentum indicators which identify overbought and oversold levels are popular among options traders" (Monna, 2021). It is important to analyze these indicators.

One will first need to understand that price rarely moves above resistance or below support. Support and resistance in technical analysis indicate the movement of the securities price where it stops then reverses to a specific price level that is often predetermined. It has a floor and ceiling.

Another thing to look at when you're doing technical analysis is moving averages, which will help you identify trends, reversals, momentum strengths, and areas where an asset will find support or resistance. The 200-day moving average is the most talked about, along with the 50 day (about 1 and a half months) moving averages. They both are worth looking at. Moving averages do not predict price direction, but they define the current direction with lag, and the averages are based on past prices, which is why they're not great as a short-term trading indicator. So you need to keep that in mind.

Another thing to look at is the Bollinger Band's standard deviation from a moving average. Many believe that the closer the price moves to the upper band, the market is overbought (Hayes, 2020). A price move outside the Bollinger Bands can signal that an asset is ripe for a reversal.

Another thing to look at is the relative strength index (RSI), a momentum indicator that measures the speed and change of price movements in a stock or any other financial asset. It moves between zero and 100, and it's considered accurate.

An RSI of above 70, is considered overbought, but when the prices are below 30 it is considered oversold which might indicate a rebound.

Another indicator to look at is the money flow index. The money flow index will measure the inflow and outflow of money into an asset over a period of 14 days. It's an indicator of trading pressure. If the indicator is over 80, it means there's a lot of more money coming in, which means the security or the stock you're interested in is overbought; if it's below 20 it indicates that it's oversold.

Intraday Momentum Index (IMI) is another important indicator that enables us to spot potential opportunities for a bullish trade in an uptrend on an intraday correction or initiate bearish trade in a down-trending market at an intraday price bump. To calculate the IMI the sum of the days is divided by the sum of the days plus the sum of the down days or ISup ÷ (ISup + IS down), which is then multiplied by 100 (Seth, 2020). While the trader can choose the number of days to look at, 14 days is the most common time frame.

Just like an RSI of 70 and above indicates that the stock is overbought and 30 indicates that the stock is oversold, the put-call ratio indicator, which we have talked about already, is one of the things you have to consider in predicting in which direction they are predicting or pinpointing an entry or an exit point.

Open interest is another important indicator that tells us how many contracts are open or unsettled. A rising price and a rising interest indicate that the market or the security is strong. A rising price and a falling open interest tell you that it is weakening. A falling price and a falling open interest tell you the market and security is strengthening.

Options Greeks

Options are presented in Greek letters, and so the options are called options Greeks because of that. Greeks explain the relationship between the contract and its underlying asset, but they are not based on real models that include real data. They are based on mathematical models that extrapolate from real data. The ones that are relevant to us are delta, gamma, theta, vega, and rho. Others exist, but they are not relevant to our decision today. Others are arcane and not beginner-friendly.

Delta Δ

$$\Delta = \frac{\partial V}{\partial S}$$

This tells us about an option's sensitivity to its underlying asset per $1 change. Call options will have a delta that ranges from 0 to 1 while put options have a delta that ranges from 0 to -1. But different platforms will present them differently, sometimes as a scale from 1 to 100, but the same principle still applies. The way to understate a delta of 0.66 is to have the option change by 66 cents for a dollar change in the underlying asset. In our case that is the stock.

Deltas keep changing as the underlying price of the stock changes, so they aren't static numbers. Deltas are higher for in the money option. For at-the-money options, they will be around 50, while the deeper the option gets in the money the more the delta increases to the 80s and higher. Sometimes it reaches a full 100, meaning it changes dollar per dollar with the stock. For out-of-the-money options, it can be as low as 20.

This number can inform a trader of what they need to do to protect themselves from risk but also spell the probability that the underlying asset will turn profitable. This all depends on the parameters set.

Gamma Γ

$$\Gamma = \frac{\partial \Delta}{\partial S} = \frac{\partial^2 V}{\partial^2 S}$$

Gamma tells us to what extent delta is sensitive to the underlying assets \$1 dollar change. It tells us at what rate the delta will change.

Gamma is higher for option on at-the-money and lover for an option out-of-the-money. The reasons for this should be obvious or will make sense later as you learn about options.

If you have an option with a call option whose underlying is trading at \$20 with a delta is 0.50 and a gamma of 0.2, it tells us that the delta of the call option will change by 20% for every 20% change in the underlying. So if the stock goes up to \$22 the delta will go up to 0.7.

Theta Θ

$$\theta = -\frac{\partial V}{\partial \tau}$$

Theta measures time decay. It tells us how much the options values will decrease as it nears its expiration date or if all things stay the same. If we have a theta value of 0.20, it tells us the price will go down by 20 cents for each day that passes. This number does not mean anything, it will depend on other parameters.

Just like gamma, theta is higher with at-the-money options and lower with on-the-money options. Some options will have negative values like puts. These numbers always change by the circumstances provided and they aren't completely set in stone.

Vega v

$$\nu = \frac{\partial V}{\partial \sigma}$$

Vega is an indicator of the options price sensitivity to its assets implied volatility. When the vega of an option is higher than the bid-ask spread, it is said that the option offers a competitive spread. Saying some have a competitive spread does not mean it is inherently a good trade to get into. As we have seen, there are other things to take into consideration when it comes to options for Greeks.

Imagine we have a call option with a bid price of $2 and an ask price of $3 and the implied volatility is 20%. If the vega is 0.40, it tells us that the bid-ask spread should look like this if the implied volatility changes by 1%: 2.40-3.40. We would also say the option is offering a competitive spread because the spread is higher than the vega.

Rho ρ

$$\rho = \frac{\partial V}{\partial r}$$

Rho gives us the sensitivity of the option price to a 1% change in interest rate. This means that an option with rho of 0.20 values at $1, then the price will increase by 20 cents if things remain the same. When it comes to a put option, they tell us how much the price will decrease and vice versa when it comes to calls. Rho is higher for at-the-money or in-the-money as opposed to those that aren't.

Chapter 5: Options Trading Strategies

We have talked an awful lot in this book about finding the right structure to match your outlook. In this chapter, we are going to explore some of those strategies. The strategies in this section will range from beginner-friendly strategies to much more complicated ones. At the end of this chapter, you should be able to pick the right strategies for the opportunities that you spot on the market. If not, you will discover a way of trading strategy that fits your style, understanding, and risk tolerance. And some of the claims that were made earlier in this book should begin to make a lot more sense as we delve deeper into these strategies, like the fact you can set the maximum profit you can get from trade and the maximum loss that you're willing to accept. It all depends on choosing the right strategy.

Naked Strategies

The first list of options trading strategies is naked strategies. We don't begin with them anymore because they are officially number one. We begin with them simply because they are the easiest to understand and they are also the riskiest of all the options trading strategies that we're going to discuss. This however does not mean they have to be neglected or rejected. They are still one of the most useful tools that the more experienced traders can use to grow their capital.

Naked strategies are used by options writers. These options writers currently do not have the resources to fulfill their end of the bargain. Remember, an option is a contract and for a contract to work somebody has to fulfill their end. Naked strategies are all about getting into a position or agreeing to terms of a contract without immediate resources to fulfill them.

Naked Call

A naked call is when an options writer writes a call option without owning the underlying stock. A call option binds the option writer to sell the underlying stock to the option holder when the option holder exercises the call option.

Normally a call option writer would own the shares that they are. They could write a call option on, for instance, 100 Coca-Cola shares, which would give an option buyer the right to buy the 100 Coca-Cola shares when they're in the money or when it's profitable for them. The assumption from the call by a specific perspective is that the call writer owns 100 Coca-Cola shares, that is why the written call option on them. A naked call option writer does not actually have 100 Coca-Cola shares to sell to the option holder.

Why would an options writer do this? Remember that option writers get to make money from the premium paid. In other words, the only money that they get is the money you pay to buy the option. So, in their heads, they're hoping that the option will expire worthlessly, and they will walk away with the premium. So you will find that the people who write naked option calls often write them on stocks that they think are a "sure thing." The risks are massive if it turns out they are wrong about their predictions. Therefore, they may want to bet on a safer stock.

Now to understand this, imagine you write a call option on 100 Microsoft shares and you sell it for about $10 per share, so you will get $1,000 if somebody buys it. Currently, Microsoft is selling at $200 per share. The call option has a strike price of $215 dollars and expires in a month. You do not expect that there will be any changes in the stock price or any large swings because Microsoft is a stable company. Now imagine what happens if, out of nowhere, Microsoft announced some groundbreaking deal with another smaller tech company that sends its stock soaring to about $250. The person who bought the call option from you will come to you asking for those 100 shares for $215 per share. You will be forced to sell them 100 Microsoft shares at $215 per share. The problem here is that you do not have those shares.

So, what do you do? To fulfill your side of the bargain, you have to go on the market and buy 100 Microsoft shares at $250 per share. You will spend $25,000 to buy 100 Microsoft shares. Then you will sell those shares for $21,500, $3,500 lower than what you spend to get them. You would lose all that money because you wanted to make a quick $1,000. You might be asking yourself, what happens if you don't have the $25,000 to buy the Microsoft shares so that you can sell them to the call option holder? Well, if you have other assets with the broker, those other assets will be liquidated to fulfill that trade. If you are holding a very good position and it is going well, you will be asked to close it or deposit money into your trading account.

As you can see, writing options and getting an option contract can be very risky.

Therefore, people who write naked call options may prefer to go for stocks that are very stable or with lower implied volatility. But if they do that, they will have to accept lower premiums. They have to also ensure that they have the funds and the resources to be able to cover that call, if the option buyer exercises their option. Naked call options are also appealing to option writers because options writers don't have to commit to a stock position to make money off a stock's movement. It's a way of being in the game without putting your skin in it. But from our example, we can see it comes with higher risks.

Most trading platforms will not allow beginners to write naked call options, but in some circumstances, if you have proven your experience and you have the funds in the capital, they may allow you to write them. However, you need to keep in mind that they can be ruinous.

Trading platforms will mostly allow beginners to write covered calls which are call options where the call writer owns the stock they're writing the option on. For instance, if you own 100 Microsoft shares, you can write a call option on them. If you own 100 Tesla shares or GameStop shares you can write 100 call options on them. Of course, that is if you own 100 shares of each. In that case, you have to make sure that you are okay with parting with 100 shares of your favorite company if the option buyer comes asking for them. If you have a long position on the stock and you're not very keen on closing it, this may be something that you don't want to do.

Naked Put Options

The naked put writer is playing a similar game to the naked call writer. Remember that a put option obliges the put writer to buy the stock from the put option buyer if the stock falls below a certain threshold. Selling a naked put option is a bit like selling insurance without having the money to cover the insured.

Now, just like our friend the call option writer, we need to ask ourselves why a put option writer would even do this. Why would you even put yourself in such a position? Well, the most obvious explanation for that is that they want to make money from the premium. As the naked put seller is very confident that the underlying stock will not fall below a certain threshold, they are happy to take the risk. Compared to the call option writer, the naked put writer is exposed to relatively less risk because the downside risk is limited. This is because stocks can go up forever, but they can only go down for so long. They stop once they hit zero and they cannot go to -$100 or anything like that. But it's still risky.

A naked put option writer might sell a naked put for Facebook shares with a strike price of $900 per share and charge a premium of $30. The put option expires within a month. Let's say the price of Facebook at the time was $950. The naked put options writer is saying they will buy 100 Facebook shares at $900 per share if the price of Facebook drops below $900. It's a promise.

And they would be very confident making that bet because who thinks Facebook's stock is going to plummet to $50 within a month? Not many people do. Facebook is a big, stable company that just keeps growing. They're relatively fewer chances that Facebook stock will go down.

Now imagine if some terrible scandal or regulation affects Facebook's business model very badly. You will see stockholders begin to sell which will drive prices down. Now, if the price of Facebook plummets to about $500 per share, the naked put option writer will be obliged to buy 100 shares from the options from the option holder at $900 per share. That's $90,000. If you don't have that kind of money, what are you going to do? The same thing we talked about with the naked call option writer will happen here with the naked pull option writer as well. You'll either have to close some of your positions to make up for that money, or you'll have to deposit money into your trading account to make up for that.

The psychology of a naked put option writing is similar to that of the naked call option writer because the writer would not go for stock that posed a greater risk to them unless they knew they could afford it or there was another play they were looking at. But there is a slight difference. As you might imagine, even if you had to spend a lot of money to buy the stock held by an option holder, at least you don't end up with nothing. You would have the stock.

Like in the last example, say you had to spend $90,000 to buy 100 Facebook shares. It might appear that you cough up $90,000 just because you wanted to make a quick $3,000. But this is not the whole picture because, in the end, you will own 100 Facebook shares. Now for the moment, those shares will be $500 per share. You have paid extra for them, but it is not over. As always with big companies, it's unlikely Facebook will plummet to zero. If you're patient enough, the company might come around. For instance, Facebook stock might struggle for a year because of new regulations but they might come up with solutions that allow them to grow again. They might acquire another company and their stock price might soar again. You will be able to sell at a profit or hold on to the stock longer. So all is not lost.

A naked call option writer will lose some of their money if the trade goes against them, and they will not have an asset in the end that can help them make it back.

Just like with naked call writers, most trading platforms will not allow beginners to write naked put options unless you have proven yourself to be proficient and able to take on the risk. Instead, most trading platforms will allow beginners to write cash-secured puts, which means every time you write a put option you have to put up the money that is needed to fulfill your side of the bargain if the option holder exercises their option. For instance, with the Facebook example, you would have to put up $90,000 in advance and that money will be held by the brokerages until the option expires worthless or the put option is exercised. This is to ensure that you will be able to meet your side of the bargain. At that stage, the brokerage does not trust you enough. You may also have to write a covered put, which we will discuss later.

Long Options

Long options are the simplest class of options strategies. In fact, we have used them to describe what options are. In this section, we're going to go through them with some concrete examples on how they would work and other considerations.

Long options are focused on the buying side of options strategies. As we've talked about earlier, going long on something is buying it or owning it in market-speak.

Long Call Option

A long call option is any option bought with the hope that the price of the underlying stock will go above the strike price. The call buyer hopes to buy the stock at a bargain before the expiration date. The upside on a call option is that the stock can go on up forever. The downside is limited to the premium paid; the premium is the only thing you lose if your bet is wrong. Long call options are fairly basic and low risk. They are basically how most traders begin trading options. This is how most imagine they will make money. They are a simple, low-risk way to make money with potentially high returns if you do it well. There aren't many threads to keep an eye on.

Long call options allow you to gain from stock's upward movement without having to put up a lot of money upfront. Here's an example to illustrate. Say you believe that Amazon stock is going to go up by about $100 per share. At present, in this fiction world, Amazon is selling $600 per share. There are two ways that we can move forward. You can buy 100 shares of Amazon for $600 per share which will cost you $60,000 and then wait until the price of Amazon goes up by $100 to $700 per share. When it reaches $700, you then sell those shares and make a profit of $10,000, not counting commission and fees. As we've seen, you had to put up a lot of capital just to see if this one bet pans out. What happens if you put up $60,000 and Amazon stock price drops to $500 per share? In that situation, you'll be forced to close at a loss of $10,000.

Of course, you don't have to sell; you could hold onto the Amazon stock and wait until something changes. But at that point, your faith in the company has probably been shattered and the chances that a company as big as Amazon will make those kinds of profits quickly are very slim.

That is the traditional way of doing it if you are a stock trader. Now, if you're an options trader and you wanted to make the same bet, it would be a lot less risky and costly for you. For instance, you would buy a call option that costs about $10 per share. That gives you the right to buy a hundred Amazon shares at $620 before the expiry date. If you buy that option contract, you spend $1,000 to make that bet. Now, if the price of Amazon does not go up by $100 like you predicted you will only lose $1,000. But if the price of Amazon goes up by $100 like you predicted you will have the right to buy those shares for $620 per share. If you want, you can sell them at once and you would have made a profit of $7,000 minus the premium.

As you can see in the second example, you only put up the big bucks when you are sure your prediction is right. You are spending your money when you have won the bet, while in the first example you begin by putting up a lot of money on a bet that could go against you and see you lose a lot of money. That's the significant difference between the two scenarios. This is what we mean when we say long call options are low risk and potentially highly rewarding since stocks can theoretically go up forever. There is no limit to how high a stock can climb (Investopedia Team, 2021).

Long call options are best used in situations where you believe the underlying stock price will go up by a significant amount, just like we have easily illustrated in the earlier example. Remember that if your bet is proven correct, you do not have to buy the shares if you don't want to; you can sell the winning contract to somebody else who's willing to spend that much money.

Long Put Options

A long-put option is when you buy a put option hoping the price of the underlying stock will fall below the strike price before expiration. Just like in the earlier example, the risk is limited to the premium that you pay for the put option. Put options give you the right to sell shares at the strike price before the expiration date. Put options are often considered the safest way to short stock.

There are two basic ways to short stock on the stock market. The first one is using stock that you own, the other is using stock that you've borrowed. For instance, if you own 100 Tesla stock and they are selling for $800 per share and you believe the price of Tesla will go down, you can sell your hundred Tesla stock on the market, wait for the price to drop, and then buy them back.

For example, if the price of Tesla drops by $100, you can buy those hundred shares back at $700.00 per share. And you would have made a profit of $10,000 from the trade because you sold them at $800 per share. There is a significant risk in doing this. Imagine what happens if instead of going down by $100, it goes up by $100. The shares you sold for $800 will now cost $900. You would be out $10,000 because you would have to buy them back at $900 per share. That's if you still want the shares. In that situation, it would have been better all along if you had just held on to your shares. Shares can rise forever. So, imagine instead of going up by $100, they go up by about $200. What are you going to do then? Because those were your shares, you can walk away and try to find another investment or cough up the money; either way.

But the second way of shorting the stock is even riskier than that because you don't use stock that you own. You pay, or sometimes put-up other kinds of collateral, to borrow stock for you. Let's say a 100 Tesla stock because you believe the price of Tesla is going to drop and then you sell those shares on the market as if they were your own. If the price of the stock goes down, it's not a problem. You buy them back and return them to their owner. The difference is you profit. The danger happens when the price goes up instead of down. In that situation, the shareowner might ask for more collateral or money for security reasons. In some situations, they can force you to return the shares back. Unlike in the earlier example, you can't just walk away from the Tesla stock. You are bound to buy those shares back at whatever price they are going for and you could lose a lot of money doing this. Short selling like this is one of the most dangerous and riskiest things anyone can do.

But there's a cheaper way to short sell, which is just to buy a put option that will give you the right to sell an underlying stock at a specific price before the expiration. Imagine you believe Tesla stock is going to go down. It doesn't matter in this scenario if you actually own the stock or if you're going to borrow it. So, Tesla is going at $800 now and you believe it'll go down by $150. So, you buy a put option for about $20 per share with a strike price of $770. That will give you the right to sell 100 shares at $770 per share, if they fall below that price. So, you put up your $2,000 to make the bet and then you just wait. If you are right in the price and the price falls to $650. Then you will sell the stock at $770 and buy it back for profit. In this situation, you didn't have to put up a lot of money to do this. Now, if your bet is wrong and Tesla soars by $300 the only thing you would've lost in that situation is the $2,000 you put up to make the bet. You don't owe anybody shares. You don't have to return your shares or somebody else's shares. You can just walk away free. Therefore, long puts are considered the safest way to short stock, whether you own the stock or plan to borrow it.

Beginner Strategies

In this section, we're going to focus on another class of beginner strategies.

Covered Call Strategy

The covered call strategy is the opposite of the naked called strategy. It involves traders selling call options on stock that they already own or selling a call option rather than buying the stock. This is to ensure that when the option holder comes asking for those shares, they can just sell the shares to the option holder. They don't have to go on the market to buy those shares and then sell them to the option holder at a loss.

Covered call strategies are the most accessible for beginners. Most trading platforms will allow new option traders to draw up covered call strategies as opposed to naked call strategies.

One of the questions we might be asking ourselves is why would an options writer draw up a covered call strategy? In the naked call example, we talked about how a call writer wanted to make money from an unlikely proposition and thus they were writing naked calls. With the covered strategy it cannot be the same or as straightforward as that because there is stock involved. The writer who writes the covered call option has stock that they might want to keep. If that is the case, why would they write a call option on a stock they don't want to lose?

There are two main reasons why a cover call writer might want to do this. I should make it clear that these are not the only reasons; they will differ by trader and what their situation is. The first most common reason is that they want to get out of the trade and make an extra buck while doing it. The second most common reason is that they want to make money off a stock that they own but does not do very much at the moment.

Let's look at this first reason:

Imagine you bought stock of company A when the company was still selling shares at $50 per share. Company A shares are now worth $100 per share. You've been holding them for a while and you don't believe that the company will grow again, but you're not sure. If you get out of this position now, you will make a profit of over 100%. You can sell a covered call option for $5 per share with the strike price of $110. If Company A goes up to $120.00 per share, you have to sell your stock for $110 per share. But when you add the $5 that you got from the premium, you are selling that stock for $115. So, you would have gotten a total of $11,500. The total amount of profit that you've made since you invested in this stock, plus the covered call option that you wrote is $6,500. Whereas if you had just sold the stock at $100, you would have made a profit of $5,000. Of course, alternatively, you could have waited until the stock rose to $120 per share, but you did not think that it would. In the scenario that the stock does not go up, like you believe it won't, you would have walked away with a profit of $5,500 if sold after expiry date. That's $500 more than you would have by just selling the stock. It is a way of making extra money on an exit.

Now, let's look at the second reason.

Owning stock can be an uneventful waiting game. It consists of periods, sometimes lasting months or years, where nothing really happens with the price of the stock. It doesn't move quickly enough in either direction. If you're confident in the company's future despite this, you might want to make extra money while you're holding the stock. You do not believe that the price of your stock will go down or up. So, writing a cover call option is a way of earning extra money on stock while you hold. You collect on the premium and don't expect that you will have to sell.

Imagine that the company's stock is at $50 per share. Since then, the stock company has grown a bit and the stock is now worth $60. Recently, the stock has been hovering between $60 and $65 and not doing much. You believe the only time the stock will rise is when the company launches a new product later in the year. Since you've predicted that, and while the company is working on their product, it'll be worth making extra money. So, you sell call options with a strike price of $68 and a premium of $2.00. That means you'll be earning

$200 on the premium. Like you predicted, nothing happens, and you make money. If you are savvy enough, you can continue doing this as the stock slowly climbs, especially if you understand the stock's growth rate and factors affecting it. You can keep on doing this and never have to sell your stock. The worst that can happen is that you are wrong, and you must sell your stock, closing your long position, but even then, it wouldn't be the end; you can still buy back your stock.

Covered Put Strategy

Basically the inverse of the cover call strategy, a covered put strategy is when a trader sells a put option and then shorts the stock in question. The trader is hoping that the price of the underlying stock will remain above the strike price, and they will collect on a premium. Since they've shorted their own stock, if the put holder exercises the put option it's not too bad because they will have the funds and it will be like they're buying their stock back. They would have made money in two ways: from shorting their own stock and from the premium. I think an example would better illustrate what we mean by this.

Let's say you own 100 shares of company Y selling at $100 per share. You do not believe that the stock price will fall. But if it falls, you want to make money from that too. So, you decide to sell a put option on company Y stock with the strike price of $90 and a premium of $5. When somebody buys the put option you will get $500 in your account. Then you will sell your hundred shares of company Y on the stock market and get $10,000 in your trading account. By opening the covered put you've received $10,500 in your account. Now, if the price of your stock stays above $90 or $100 you do not have to worry about the option holder exercising the option. After the expiry date, you can either buy your stock back at the same price that you sold it or at a little less than what you sold it for. If the price drops to $95 per share that means you will buy back your stock for $9,500 and you would have made $1,000 in profit from both the premium and from shorting the stock.

In another scenario, if the price of the stock plummets to $70 per share, the put option holder will exercise their put option and you'll be obliged to buy 100 shares from them at $90 per share. Meaning $9,000 will be deducted from your account. From the premium, you would have made $500. At the end of the day, you'll have your stock back. So it's not too bad.

If you are right in your prediction and the stock goes up by $5, it will be $105. You would have the money to buy a hundred shares back at the price. If the stock blows up even more than the premium you got when you opened the position, you might find yourself having to buy back the stock at a much higher price than you would like. In that situation, it would be up to you if you want to buy the stock back or leave it and look for another opportunity. A covered put is safer because it ensures that you have the funds to fulfill your obligation of the put. Just like the covered call strategy.

Cash Secured Put Strategy

Cash secured put is when an investor sells a put option and then sets the money aside to cover their side of the bargain. The person who writes the cash-secured put strategy believes the stock will rise, perhaps it will dip for a little while but it will rise again.

So a cash-secured put strategist is looking for stock to invest in, but they're not comfortable with buying it at the price it is selling at currently. So, they wait for a temporary dip and then get in on the stock. They hold until the stock goes up again. They could decide to watch the stock and then place an order when the dip happens, but there's no guarantee that when they place an order that they will get the stock at a specific price. All sorts of things can happen; it could experience price slippage, or you might not get the number of shares you want. So, writing a put option like this is a way of securing the number of shares you want at the price you want. Once the stock price dips below the strike price the option holder will exercise their put option. You will buy those shares at the agreed-upon price, without any friction or complications. It makes things smoother and easier. That's one of the reasons why cash-secured puts work.

For instance, let's see you are keen on getting on Amazon stock which is selling at $200 per share currently but you're not willing to buy Amazon shares at $200 per share. You're confident that Amazon will do well, and it's going to be worth a lot more in the future. So, you write a put option with the strike price of $180 because you're comfortable paying that much. Let's say the premium is $5 per share. You sell that and then you wait. If the price of Amazon temporarily slips because of bad press or some other controversy, say it dips to $150, the put option holder will exercise their put option and you will get the number of shares you want at a price you want. In this scenario, you've written a put option, which essentially locks the price at $180 per share. That's the beauty of a cash secured put.

Married Put/Protective Put

A married put or protective put is another popular strategy. I've talked about it earlier when I was describing put options. If you remember earlier, I talked about how put options are like insurance. Essentially that's how married put works. It is a strategy that investors holding stock use for hedging their positions.

So, let's say you've invested in a company and this company is doing very well. You bought your first shares for $100, and everything seems to be going well. Now the company stock is valued at $150 per share. You're worried that this is unsustainable, that it will go down. There is an upcoming company event and sales announcement and you think, because of the pandemic, that it isn't going to be good and might translate into a sell-off, meaning the price will plummet. But you're also hopeful that it will be good news and it will send the stock to new heights. So, what do you do to protect the winnings you've already acquired? You can buy a put option with a strike price of $145 for a premium of $6. It will cost you $600 If it's only 100 shares. If the stock goes up, you are happy. If you're right and the stock goes down, you can sell those shares for $145 per share, which would be above market value at the time that you exercise your put option. Just like that, you would have secured some of the profit you've made from your long position.

Investors holding the married put option don't want the stock to go down. They're buying the put option as insurance.

Collar

The protective collar is a combination of a put option and a call option. Investors do this when they are worried something might happen in the stock market that might negatively affect their long position. So what they do is write a call option on stock they hold and then buy a put option on the same stock. Both options share the same expiration date and the same underlying stock.

The protective collar caps your profits on the long position and limits your losses. Your profits are kept at the premium and the strike price of your call option minus the premium that you paid. The protective collar also limits the amount of loss from your long position to the put option's strike price and the premium paid.

The collar works when both the put option and the call option are out-of-the-money. Collars are a cost-effective strategy than just buying a protective put or a married put. The protective collar is best to use when the market has been bullish and as an investor, you are worried about a correction. Now let's look at an example to illustrate how this works.

Say, you own 100 shares of Sony and Sony has been going through a terrific rise to about $250 per share. You have reason to believe that there might be a decline soon, so you want to protect the gains that you've already made in the stock. But you also don't want to pay a high price for a premium on the protective put. So, you sell a call option on the stock with a strike price of $255 and a premium of $3 per share. So you will get $300 credited into trading your account. Then you buy a put option with a strike price of $245 that costs $3 per share. So, you take the $300 you got from selling the call option and use it to buy the put option.

If the put option costs more than the premium that you got from selling your call option, you've reduced the price by on the put premium. If you're right and the stock falls below the $245 you will exercise your put option and sell your stock at $245 per share and you would have paid nothing for the protection. That's the maximum you can get from this position. The downside is if you're wrong and the stock rallies again. Let's say it rises to about $260. The person you saw the call option will exercise their option. You will sell your stock at $255 per share and forego the extra $5 profit. That's the worst that can happen in this scenario.

You have kept the gains from your long position. You got yourself protection at a bargain. Therefore, the protective color is one of the most favored strategies when investors fear correction in the near term.

Buying LEAPS

LEAPS are perfect for risk-averse investors. They are used in two basic ways. The first one is to protect against a market correction that you are. For instance, you can buy a put LEAP on the number of shares you are longing for the long term, whether that is one, two, or three years. The second way of using LEAPs is for putting stock on layaway or locking it for purchase at a particular time in the future without having to put up all your money upfront. Just like we have talked about in the long call example.

LEAPs come in both call options and put options. They are the same as regular options. The main difference is that they expire in more than a year to about three years. They can be used in similar ways that we've talked about options. They have costlier premiums, and they are less sensitive to movement in underlying assets.

Choosing the Right Strategy

There isn't one best or great strategy to use. A strategy is only as good as it helps with your goals. So when picking a strategy, you should think about how it will fit into your goals. For instance, if you want to protect your investment a married put will make more sense to you.

As a beginner, it makes more sense for you to use simpler strategies and get good at them. Only later when you have built your experience as an options trader can you begin trying more advanced strategies. The strategies discussed here will go a long way, but you are not losing anything by not trying advanced strategies. A strategy is only as good as how it's being used. So as a trader you shouldn't think more advanced strategies are inherently desirable or better than just sticking with the simple ones. How a strategy is used is more important than what the strategy is.

That is the one rule you need to follow.

More Advanced Strategies

Let's spend the rest of the chapter looking at some of the more advanced options trading strategies. These are the kinds to try after you have perfected the more beginner-friendly strategies.

Bear Call Spread Strategy

The bear call strategy involves writing a call option and buying a call option on the same underlying security with the same expiry date. Both calls have the same number of underlying shares, so if you write two calls you buy two calls.

In this strategy, the trader believes the price of the underlying security will fall, so they want to profit from that and also limit their risk. The strategy also limits the reward. The maximum amount that can be made from the strategy is from the premiums received when opening the position. Let's turn to an example to illustrate.

Say ADV stock is selling at $30 per share. You wire an expensive in-the-money call option with a strike price of $28 and a premium of $4. Then buy a cheaper out-of-the-money for call option at $1 with a strike price of $32. You will get $400 from the call you sold and then spend $100 to buy a call option. This will make your profit $300. That is the maximum you can make from this position.

If the price of ADV goes down as you predicted there is nothing to worry about; your strategy has worked as planned and both options expire worthless. If the price of ADV goes up to $40 for unforeseen reasons your maximum loss on this position will be the difference between the two strike prices and minus the credit/profit received, which is $100. Here is how we got to that number: $28,00 – 32,00 = 400, 400 – 300 = 100. But why?

When the price of the stock is suddenly above $32, the call option holder will exercise their call option which will prompt you to buy 100 ADV shares and sell them. But instead of buying them at $40, you will exercise your call option and buy them for $3,200. When you sell them you will receive $2,800. Since you had $300 credited into your account, you have only been set back $100 from your total balance. You sold those shares for $3,100 when you bought them at $3,200. As you can see this is what is meant when we say it is a limited risk and reward strategy; you can only make so much and lose so much.

When dealing with spread, volatility is one of the things to keep in mind because it can affect both options differently.

Bear Put Spread Strategy

The trader who uses this strategy believes the stock will fall. It works by selling an out-of-the-money put option while buying an in-the-money put option, on the same underlying stock with the same expiry date. The maximum profit that can be made from this is equal to the difference between the strike prices minus how much it cost to set it up.

Say ADV is trading at $40 per share. You are convinced that the price of the stock will go down. So, you have an expensive in-the-money put option for $6 with a strike price of $44. Then you sell an out-of-the-money put option for $2, with a striker price of $39. You would have paid a maximum of $400 to set up the whole strategy. If the price of AVD finished below $38, the put option holder will exercise their put option. Buying those shares will cost you $3,800 and then you will sell those shares for $4,400. Since it cost you $400 to set up the whole strategy your profit is $200. If the price of ADV finishes above your striker price you have lost all your money and see no profits. If it is finished in between, your profit will be reduced. The main aim of this strategy is to reduce the amount it takes to buy the in-the-money put option.

The Bull Call Strategy

The bull spread strategy is used when the trader believes the underlying asset will appreciate in value, but the trader wants to limit the amount they spend on the call option. They do this by buying and selling a call option on the same underlying security with the same expiry date and the same number of shares. This has the effect of limiting losses and gains.

Say you are a trader looking at ADV, which is trading at $50 per share. The trader believes ADV will go up in value within a month because of the upcoming company event, which is bound to be exciting. So, they sell a call option for $2 with a strike price of $60. Then they buy a call option with a strike price of $51 for $3. The sale of their call option cuts their costs by $2, meaning they only spend $1 for their call options. As soon as the stock rises above $51 it is profitable for them to exercise their call option. But their games are capped when the stock reaches $60.

Imagine ADV stock reaches $100. In that scenario they would buy a hundred shares for $5,100 and then sell them to the option holder for $6,000, making a profit of $900 minus the premium paid. If they didn't sell the call option, they would have benefited from the extra $40 increase in the stock.

If the stock plummets because of a disastrous event, both options expire worthless but the trader has lost $100, not the $300 he would have lost if he bought the call option alone. As you can see, the risk and the profit are capped.

Bull Put Spread Strategy

In this strategy, the trader believes the underlying stock will rise. The strategy is initiated by buying an out-of-the-money put option while selling an in-the-money put option, on the same security which shares the same expiry date. By now you should be able to figure out how most credit spreads. Let's turn to an example to make things even simpler.

Let's say that GM is selling at $50 per share and you are confident that the stock will go up as there is an upcoming earnings announcement and the company has been doing well since int's inception. So, you sell an in-the-money put option for $5 with a strike price of $52. Then you buy an out-of-the-money put option for $2 with a strike price of $47. You will get a $300 net credit. That is the maximum profit you can make from this position.

If the price of the stock goes up, you will have made your maximum profit. If the price of the stock plummets to $39, the option holder will exercise their option and you will have to buy the 100 shares at $5,200. Then you would sell those shares at $47 by exercising your call option. You will get $4,700 Because you had $300 credited to your account you have lost $200 on the trade, not the full $500 difference between the two striker prices. But things would have been worse without your second put option which capped your losses. This strategy has the same effect as others we have discussed in this section, they cap losses and rewards. A trader already knows the maximum profit and the maximum loss each position poses.

The Straddle

The straddle is another options trading strategy. It is very effective when you are expecting the underlying stock will have a significant price movement, but you're not sure in which direction: up or down. The straddle involves buying a put option and a call option on the same underlying asset with the same expiry date. Profit is realized when the stock moves significantly enough to cover the premiums that you've paid. In rare circumstances, both options can become profitable. Usually only one of them will. Here's a quick example to illustrate.

Imagine that you've been watching Apple stock which has been trading at $200 per share. There's an upcoming Apple event, and you expect it to be either a very exciting announcement or one that will fail to impress investors and could result in a price dive. While you cannot be certain what direction the stock will go, and the fundamentals cannot tell you enough, you do know that the stock price is going to move significantly, and you want to profit from that movement. So, you initiate a straddle strategy. You buy a call option at $3 with a strike price of $200. You buy a put option with a strike of $200 that costs $3. At this point, you have spent $600 to open this position. This means you'll only begin making a profit when the stock rises or falls by more than $6. For instance, if it falls to $193.99 or below, you can begin to exercise your put option at profit. The same thing applies if the stock reaches $206.01. That is because at those prices the initial $600 you paid is covered.

In most circumstances, the stock is only going to go in one direction, and that's going to be it. For instance, if the Apple event goes very well, the stock rises perhaps to $250 per share. Your call option will be immensely profitable. But it's very unlikely that the opposite will happen before the option expires. If the event does not go well Apple stock will fall, making your put option profitable.

In very rare circumstances, where the stock is very volatile, it can go down to about $180, making your put option profitable and then go up, making the call option profitable. The struggle has that advantage to it. But the disadvantage is that opening this position is expensive and the price must move a lot more before you turn a profit. If none of them pan out, you lose way more money than you would have lost if you're just betting on one outcome.

The Strangle

This strangle is the last options strategy we will talk about. It is the cousin of the straddle strategy, and it comes in two flavors: the long strangle and the short strangle. The main difference between the straddle and the strangle is that the strangle involves the use of out-of-the-money options while the straddle involves the use of at-the-money options. Let's explore the long and the short strangle below.

Long Strangle

In the long strangle the investor believes the underlying stock will move widely in opposite directions, meaning there is potential for them to earn money on both the downswing and the upswing. To profit from this movement they buy an out-of-the-money put option and a call option on the same underlying asset with the same expiry date and involving the same amount of shares.

Imagine you have been watching IBM stock and you believe that because of current market conditions the stock is very volatile. The stock is currently trading at $100. So you buy a put option for $4 with a strike price of $95. Then you buy a call option with a strike price of $105 for $4. Opening this position, you have spent $800, which is the maximum you stand to lose on this trade. The stock has to rise and fall by more than $8 for you to start seeing profit from this position. If IBM's stock acts like you predicted and falls to $90, you can exercise your put option or sell the put option for a profit. If next week the stock continues to be volatile and goes up to $115 your call option is profitable, and you can exercise it or sell it. The long strangle only works if the stock moves wildly. If it moves to both strike prices and recedes you can break even. If it moves in one direction to the strike price and recedes to the current price you would have lost $400.

Short Strangle

The short strangle is used when an investor believes the underlying stock will meander between two price points and will not go above them. It is best for relatively stable stocks. The investors sell an out-of-the-money put option and an out-of-the-money call option on the same stock, sharing the same expiry and the same number of shares.

Take our IBM example, let's say the stock has been meandering between $94 and $106. The investors may sell a put option with striker price of $93 and a call option with striker price of $107 for $3 each. That means they will get a $600 net premium credited into their account. That is the maximum they can make from this position. Their losses on the upside are unlimited and their losses on the downside are limited to how far the stock can fall. If things go as predicted they walk away with $600.

Imagine if the IBM stock goes up by $150 because they have invented some new technology. The investor will have to buy that stock to sell or buy back their position at a high price, approximately $3,700. That is because they would have to buy the stock at $150 per share ($15,000) and sell it for $107 per share, losing $4,300. When you subtract the premium the total goes down to $3,700. However, traders don't have to do this dance; they can buy back their call option for $4,300. If the stock falls below the put strike price, to $70, they would lose $1,700.

As you can see, the upside risk on this trade is unlimited, because the price of the stock can continue rising and the holder might want to hold out until they are satisfied with a larger profit. This is a far riskier strategy than the long strangle. The long strangle limits the risk to the premium you pay.

Rolling Options

As you trade, you will hear of traders rolling options. Traders roll an option to continue a winning position, to improve a position, or another goal. We will go through some of the common scenarios and explore the three types of rolling options below.

Rolling Up

Rolling up is when you replace a lower strike option with a higher strike option. They are more common with call options, and there are a couple of situations where they are warranted.

For instance, if you bought a call option and the stock is moving in a higher direction, you might want to close out your initial call option and buy another higher strike call option so you can continue making profit from the same strategy. Instead of waiting until the stock price is very high and exercising your call option, you lock in the little profit you've made now and open another option.

This works the same way we've talked about earlier about not staying in positions too long just because they're going in your direction. Instead of waiting to double or even triple your profits, you should close the position and roll up the option.

Imagine you bought a call option of Intel with a strike price of $70 that expires within three months, within the first month something unexpected happens and the price of Intel goes up by 10%. Already you've made a 10% profit. The right thing to do is to close your position. But because the stock is not showing any signs of slowing down, you roll up by buying another call option at a higher strike price. For instance, you buy a call option with a strike price of $78. This has a couple of benefits. If the stock went up and down again and you didn't exercise your first call option, you would have lost money on the first call option's premium. In the second case, if the stock goes up and down again, you will have only lost money on your second option, but you would have collected profit on your first option.

Rolling Down

Rolling down mostly deals with put options. They're usually put in action when a trade has gone in your favor very quickly and you want to preserve some of the profits made.

For instance, you buy a put option and it does well. Instead of watching the stock for more profit, you roll down by getting another option with a lower strike price. It's similar to rolling up but in the opposite way.

You bought a put option for Coca-Cola at the strike rate of $100 that lasts a month and then within the first week, Coca-Cola drops by $20 from $110 and now you've made more than 10% profit. You thought it wouldn't happen that quickly and it looks like that it is going to keep on falling. So, to minimize the risk and continue your winning trajectory, you close out this option and buy another put option at the strike rate of $85. That is called rolling down. This has two effects. If the price of Coca-Cola goes up again and you didn't exercise the first put option, you will lose the premium. If you rolled down and the same thing happened, you would still have taken profit from my first option and lost some money on your second option. Not too bad.

Rolling Out

Rolling out is when a trader replaces an option with an identical option at the end of the first option's expiry date. Traders might even do it before the end date of the first option and opt for another option with a longer time span. The purpose of rolling out is to secure more time for a thesis to play out. For instance, you might have bought a call option expecting that a company's stock will rise by a certain percentage, and it looks like things are moving in that direction, but they're moving very slowly than you had expected. Your call option is about to expire. Instead of just closing out your position at a loss, you open another position that's identical to the one you already have with a longer expiration date so that the stock has more time to move in the direction you hope.

So, imagine that you bought a Qualcomm call option with a strike price $107, and at present, Qualcomm is selling at $98 per share. The option expires in a month and within that time the price of Qualcomm moves to about $104. Instead of just giving up and walking away, you sell your option and open another position that is identical to the first with a longer or same expiration date. That's what rolling out is. It works the same way with put options; you buy another put option. It's about adding more time to the option or position.

This usually happens when a trader is confident in their thesis and they're seeing it play out, so they stick to it. The obvious concern is that you might be chasing a trade that has lost, instead of accepting your loss and moving on. Anything can happen in the stock market; if a trade is looking favorable it does not mean it will stay that way or it is following some secret pattern you have unlocked. There aren't rules a stock has to follow, clear patterns only exist in hindsight.

Automating Your Trading

Trading is really hard. I am not going to lie to you about it. Options trading is even harder. That is because there is a lot more to think about than if it were just stocks alone. So how do you overcome that? There are a couple of ways to do this. First, you can do the hard work yourself and build your experience, but that can take a lot of time and you could use a lot of money. You might find that it is not for you. This applies regardless of whether you are a complete beginner or you have some trading experience. Secondly, you might just want someone else to trade for you: that is what automatic trading is.

Automatic trading will involve an individual or a firm that specializes in trading for other people. So, they will learn about your goals and needs and then identify opportunities for you based on them. They do the hard work of fundamental analysis and technical analysis and make trades on your behalf with your permission, on your trading account. You will have to inform your broker about this. You will still be able to access your account and monitor it. Automatic trading is all about taking the hard work and emotions out of the game. Letting an expert in the field bear the weight.

Automatic training is sometimes compared to having a financial advisor who also executes the trades. In this instance, the financial advisor won't be communicating every move that they make with you. This sounds like a great deal, especially if you are not confident about your knowledge and tend to be risk-averse. Giving your money to an automatic trader is not risk-free; losing your money is always possible. Those needs and goals are balanced with risks.

Like I said, they aren't just a solution for new inexperienced investors, seasoned traders use them too. There are a few reasons why seasoned traders might want to do this. One is that they are not knowledgeable in the security or industry they want to invest in. Secondly, they may not have the time and energy to pour their souls into it. Thirdly, they may want another eye to help them with their trading.

There are many services out there that offer automatic trading. I am not talking about auto trading software that uses algorithms to trade; these are incredibly difficult to use, even if they appear easy to set up. They are difficult to get right. How a human thinks and the assumptions they make is not how a computer thinks, meaning you might be configuring it in a way that doesn't fit with your goals. As low as 5% of the people who opt for auto trading software are successful. So, when looking for a service, explicitly specify you are looking for a human or firm to help you with your portfolio and then instruct your broker to give them control of your account.

Many brokerages offer auto trading themselves, they will run your account for you and you will watch your trades from the comfort of your home and interject or ask questions where you need clarifying. Brokerages will charge extra fees for this service. These services also come in tiers that offer different levels of involvement and care.

You can ask your brokerage if they have one or if they have good recommendations for you.

The popular kind of auto trading is newsletter recommendation auto trading. This is where you and a service make an agreement that they will send newsletters alerts and trade recommendations to your brokerage to be executed by the broker as specified in a newsletter you subscribe to. You can set parameters with the service provider, like what percentage of the trade you want executed at a time. This takes the hard work of going into your inbox, reading a trading strategy, and executing it yourself out of the equation. Another alternative is portfolio management services.

Portfolio management services are much more comprehensive and come in different forms. Active portfolio management is where a manager actively tries to generate higher returns for your portfolio. They will try more risky strategies while also trying to curb risk through methods like diversification. Passive portfolio management will try to generate returns from safer, more stable investments. They will deal with index funds and other low return but stable investments. This type of wealth building is much more suitable for long-term goals.

Then there is discretionary portfolio management where the manager has full control of the investor's account and makes decisions for them based on their goals and risk tolerance. Before an arrangement like this takes place, the manager will have discussions with the client that will form the basis for the strategies and methods they will implement. Then there is non-discretionary portfolio management, in this instance, the portfolio manager functions more like an advisor than a trader, they guide the investor based on their goals and risk tolerance. As you can imagine the more active and involved types of portfolio management are expensive and usually require a hefty sum to open an account, sometimes as high as $100,000.

If you don’t feel the need and are ready to take the plunge and you have the money, you can opt for services like these which can trade options for you while you take care of other business. They are not viable solutions for those without the money.

Chapter 6: Beyond Stocks

As we have already discussed in earlier chapters you can trade options whose underlying assets aren't stocks. Indexes and ETFs are some of the other alternatives. We will discuss why they may be appropriate for beginners too.

ETF Options

Exchange-traded funds (ETFs) are index funds that trade like stocks on the stock market. They are highly liquid, meaning investors can opt-in and out of them fairly easily. Just like stocks, you buy shares of exchange-traded funds. The appeal of ETFs is that they take demanding work out of investing in a particular industry or market by bundling up shares and assets which track the performance of that segment of market or industry. They come in different flavors, from highly risky ones to fairly safe.

It's easier for analysts and traders to predict how an industry will perform than it is to predict which companies within that industry will be successful. So bundling up shares that mimic an industry gives traders and analysts much more predictive power. Compared to market indexes there are many more ETFs, with some more specialized than others. For instance, you can get one that's solely focused on emerging markets, the technology sector, or S&P 500. This allows investors to further specify what segment of a market they want to invest in and gauge their risk.

As we've talked about, it is especially important to focus on options that have a high trading volume as opposed to those that don't have it. High trading volume shows the asset is highly liquid, meaning there won't be any problem opening and closing positions. Here's a list of options that have high trading volume:

SPDR S&P 500 (SPY)

iShares Russell 2000 Index Fund (IWM)

PowerShares QQQ Trusts (QQQQ)

iShares MSCI Emerging Markets Index (EEM)

SPDR Dow Jones Industrial Average ETF (DIA)

Market Vector Semiconductors ETF (SMH)

ETF options are much more attractive because they're simpler to predict. For instance, if there is news that a supposed change will impact an industry negatively, you'll be able to predict a downside movement in that industry. However, there will be some companies in that industry who will rise above it and actually do better than the average. Figuring out which ones will be able to thrive in those conditions is a lot more difficult and requires extensive fundamental analysis and research.

Take cryptocurrencies for example. It is much easier for us to say that news of countries accepting one of them as a legal tender will affect the market positively. Any tracker of cryptocurrencies will see a rise. But it will be difficult to predict which coins are going to benefit from that news. For instance, you might find that Bitcoin takes a dive while Ethereum and a handful of others see a rise. The same applies to ETFs. If you understand the industry, market, and the types of assets that are bundled within an ETF, you can be fairly consistent.

How to Use ETF Options

Here are some of the ways that you can use your ETF options. You can use them to earn and enhance the performance of your portfolio. You can use them to hedge downside risk, selling options for extra income, or to gain access to sectors and markets. ETF options work well with buy-write and covered calls strategies.

Index Options

Index options are another class of options that are easier for beginners to use. ETFs sell shares that are bundled up to track an index option. When the index option is exercised at expiry (the only time you can exercise it) there's nothing that exchanges hands except money.

ETFs sell shares that are bundled up to track an index option. Indexes are analytical tools made of a hypothetical share portfolio. For instance, imagine that you have a 100 ETF shares contract. When the contract is exercised, 100 shares will exchange hands (money for shares, shares for money). But index options are like bets because there are no shares that exchange hands when an option is exercised. The only thing that exchanges are money. If your position is proved right you are paid, when you are wrong about the premium, you don't get paid.

Index options are preferred by some traders because there's nothing extra to manage except the option itself. You don't have to worry about shares or another underlying asset. All you are betting on is how theoretical index shares will perform. It saves on transaction cost and is favorable for tax treatment.

How to Use Index Options

Index options are primarily used to bet on an index. As we have already talked about, it's easier to predict the behavior of a group of assets than it is to predict one company. You can use them to collect on an income based on a mild directional view of the Nasdaq-100 index in the future. You can also use them to hedge a portfolio against looming market correction. Index options are one of the most popular options trades because they are not as volatile as individual stocks. As we have already established when deciding whether you're going to go with any tier foreign index options, you need to think about the trading volume. It's important that there's high trading volume because that means there's higher liquidity and so it's important especially when it comes to ETFs and Index options.

Compound Options

Compound options are options on options, a derivative on a derivative. As soon as I said this you might have asked yourself 'why?' We will get to that. I know as regular everyday traders we hate making things more complicated than they need to be; however, as you'll see compound options might be an exception.

Compound options give the owner the right to buy or sell an option. There are two striker prices and expiry dates. Compound options come in four types. You have a call option on a put option, which is abbreviated CoP. This option gives you the right to buy a put option. The second option is the put on a put option; it is abbreviated PoP. It gives you the right to sell a put option. The third option is the call on a call option, which is abbreviated CoC or CaCall; it gives you the right to buy a call option. Lastly, we have the put option on a call option, which abbreviated PoC; it gives you the right to sell a call option.

In this instance, the terminology changes a bit to avoid confusion. For instance, the premium you pay for the compound option is called the back fee and the compound option is called the overlying while the second option is underlying.

Compound options are generally European style, meaning they can only be exercised on the expiration day. These options are more popular in European exchanges than in the U.S. The reason compound options are used is because they allow the trader to ride an asset at a much cheaper price than buying a regular option. It is a way of getting your nose in without committing. But if the trader decides to exercise it usually costs them more than if they had just bought the vanilla option.

Binary Options

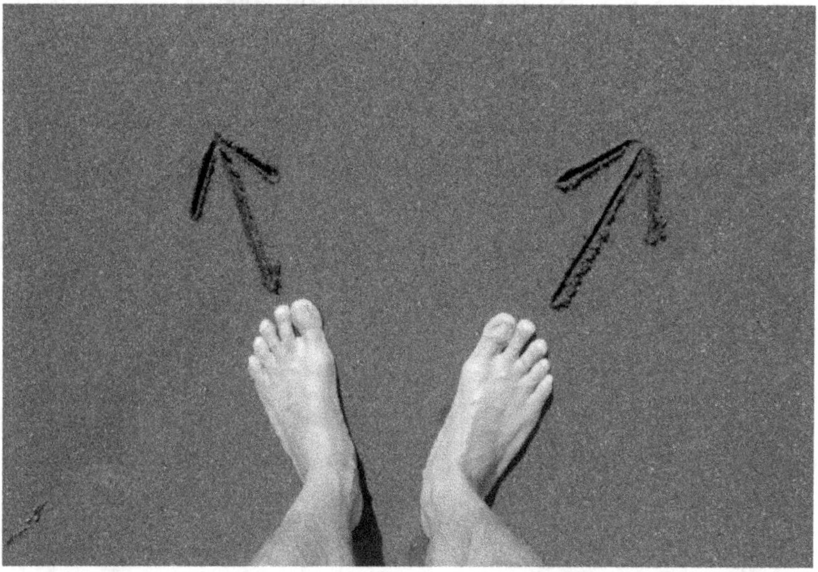

Earlier I talked about options not being a zero-sum game, but there is one exception: binary options. Binary options are one of the easiest to understand and take part in. Binary options, as the name hints, are true or false/yes or no propositions. A trader who buys a binary option believes something will happen and the trader who sells the binary options believes it won't—no ifs or buts.

Binary options are always priced between $0 to $100 and traders that only make between $0 to $100 per option contract. Binary options are not exercised; they expire and are then settled. Binary options inherently cap risk and reward. They are traded on the Nadex exchange.

Here is how a binary option will work. The binary option is posed like a question, like "Do you think the S&P will be above $1,500 at 12 p.m. this Friday?" This is presented like this: S&P 500 > $1,500 12pm. Then there will be a bid and ask price. If you believe the S & P 500 will be above $1,500 at 12 pm on Friday, you will buy the option and if you believe it won't you will sell the option. If you are a seller, you would put money aside to settle your side of the bargain. The bid and ask will both be between $0 and $100. It might look like this: bid $30 and ask $70. If you buy the binary option, you pay $30. If you are right the seller will pay up to $70. If you are wrong, you have lost $30, and the seller keeps the money. You can buy as many binary options as you like on the same proposition, as many as the other party is willing to sell to maximize your profit, while simultaneously increasing the amount of risk you are exposed to.

On the Nadex exchange, indices are often the ones being traded. So, if you want to trade in binary options you will have to choose an index you are confident about predicting and understanding. The exchange also offers others like currencies and commodities. If you are comfortable in any of these, they might be worth giving a shot.

In the example above, I have simplified the scenario by removing fees that the exchange charges for each contract, just like I have done in the rest of the book with all the other options we have been talking about. Binary options can be closed at any time to take profit or minimize loss.

Chapter 7: Trends in Trading

A lot of the advice that I've given in this book has been very traditional and, in some sense, normal. But in this day and age, a trader has to think about more than just the old ways of doing what's been done. A lot is changing. These are not normal times in the financial world and have introduced a new kind of risk or conditions that we as traders have to think about before we make any decisions in the financial markets.

I'm going to describe what the situation is and what some of the proposed approaches to it are. And I'm hoping you will be able to make up your mind about the merits of all of these different approaches to this situation. That you'll be able to make good decisions for yourself.

I've mentioned the topic of this chapter earlier in this book chapter. Here, I would like to go deeper into it.

The Meme-Fication of Trading

The popularization of trading through the introductions of free apps made the trading experience a lot easier and more accessible for anyone to trade, younger generations in particular. This, along with other developments in the tech sphere, has led to the rise of meme stocks. Usually, meme stocks are described as trading without regard for the securities fundamentals. This trading, which usually involves sending stocks higher, happens because of more social reasons, a joke, or some narrative that younger generations find compelling.

I think a much easier way of understanding it is by describing it as social media-driven trading which results in mania. It's trading that is almost completely based on sentiment, with little consideration of the facts/fundamentals.

A description like that might be unfair because in these circles where retail investors come together and reflect on the markets, there's a lot of discussion about the fundamentals, stocks, strategies, and how retail investors can improve themselves as traders and investors. And there's a lot of learning going on. If it wasn't for this market or phenomena, this book wouldn't have the kind of value it does today. There's a hunger for information about markets and trading today; it's at an all-time high.

So this meme-ry is not totally unmoored from any kind of reasoning or sophistication. It's not a bunch of crazy people coming together and deciding they want to screw over the markets or anything like that. But because social media-driven investing is informed by things such as Reddit, Twitter, and TikTok, it can mean that stocks get pumped, and for no apparent reason when you look at the fundamentals or coverage concerning the company of business.

Here's why this is a problem for regular and retail investors out there. For the first time in our lives, just looking at the stocks fundamentals and other relevant information is not enough. This all means we have to look above and beyond all we are used to, although it's not that we haven't been doing this all along. Before the advent of social media, we as traders have always been thinking about ways that we can read the markets that extend beyond what traditional information is telling us. We will think about politics, what's happening in society, what the economy looks like, what the public's attitude is, and a lot of other factors.

So looking beyond the numbers, company records, research, and analysis have always been something that we do. And it has allowed us to stave off a lot of unpredictability in the markets. Meme stocks bring a whole new dimension to this. They add another layer which is complex and can make meme stocks difficult to predict. Unless you are on those platforms, Reddit, TikTok, etc., you cannot be certain that the stocks that you're interested in will behave the way that you expect them to just based on the numbers alone and traditional sources of information. Sure, there are many stocks out there that go untouched by the meme stock crowd, but meme stocks can turn to or touch any stock in the market. It depends on what the prevailing narrative is, what 'finfluencers' are saying and the mood in WallStreetBets-like communities.

I should make it clear that I do not disparage or think that these communities or meme-fication crowd are a bunch of clueless people. I don't think so. This chapter is as much for them as it is for everyone else. At the end of the day, we are all playing the same game.

It's just that meme stocks introduces a whole dimension of risk, but is also a wonderful thing to see happening. So this is the situation. There has been a lot of talk about how to approach this situation. Let's talk about those ideas and then you can make up your own mind.

Just Avoid Meme Stocks

The assumption here is that meme stocks are inherently dangerous so you should avoid them if you want to make money. I want to get into this advice by exploring two things: the ways meme stocks are dangerous and how to avoid them.

Meme stocks are vulnerable to pump and dump schemes or the pump and dump phenomenon. What do I mean by that? A pump and dump scheme is suggesting an organization or a group of people who are somehow affiliated who come together and decide to pump stock for a profit. But what's happening with meme stocks is not a pump and dump scheme in the literal sense that we use it, or at least there's a possibility that it isn't. When you think of the people on Reddit forums or Twitter or TikTok, what you're seeing is a bunch of people giving each other advice. They like a particular stock and then they pile onto that stock because it interests them or it's super convincing for them. Then you see the stock rise and there will be advice on these forums about holding to the stock or they encourage each other to keep buying. There's a lot of excitement about it, and it's a bit like a game in a community of people who are just doing something fun and insane.

There isn't a sense in which these people are intentionally trying to pump stock, although they share the same goals. Granted, there might be some people in there who have a lot of friends who are taking advantage of a lot of other traders with little knowledge through this kind of environment. But it is likely in most circumstances, it's just something that's more organic like a Twitter trend. Even if this is the case, what we have in the end is a pump and dump phenomenon that's dictated by the sentiment of all traders in these communities. It always ends with some people losing a lot of money and some making a lot of money. But mostly it ends up in losses because there are far more sophisticated traders who can take advantage of the situation.

But there is also a chance that they could be orchestrating pump and dump schemes that don't happen in the same way that we're used to. It could be that you have bots on Twitter or in some forums that are hyping stock to a lot of unsuspecting users who may jump on that stock, driving prices high. And the rest is history. Some users have the power and expertise to do that. The same way companies can get a social media hashtag trending, the same can be done for stocks and other financial assets.

Both things are true: you can have stocks that behave like pump and dumps schemes because of simple psychological reasons, or you can have one that's orchestrated by tech-savvy individuals.

So those are the reasons why meme stocks are dangerous. Now let's turn to the second part of the argument, which is that you should avoid them. This is part of the advice that presupposes that you can always know when a stock is a meme stock. The list of meme stocks changes all the time. The mainstays right now are GameStop, AMC, and Nokia, but any stock can catch the attention of the meme crowd for a lot of unknown reasons. Those reasons are inherently unpredictable. You don't know where the conversations in those communities will go and what might be the next exciting thing. You have no idea what Michael Burry or Elon Musk will tweet, who are both very influential people in these communities. And you don't know how it might affect your stock and therefore your options. So, the idea only works to the extent that you already know what stocks are hot with the memers. So, if you want to avoid a pump and dump risk, you have to keep in mind that they change all the time.

Good advice or bad advice? I don't know.

Embrace the Change

This is the advice that goes, "Don't try to avoid the wave, soon we will all be wet, and you have to learn how to ride those waves now." The belief is that what we are seeing now is the beginning of a seismic shift in finance, much like we saw in retail. Retail investors have so much power and control that they will be the ones calling the shots. In other words, disruption is coming for wall street. It is not as if we don't see these changes starting to take place coupled with the threat of cryptos to the financial system as we know it.

Since the world is changing it is much better to become a part of that learning change, to learn how to navigate your way through it instead of completely avoiding it. In the end, you are going to live in that world so start now. There is some truth in that idea and I lean towards it.

There is value in being a part of those online communities, seeing how and what they think but don't forget to also be doing your own study, research, and making trades based on your resulting outlook. You might find you disagree with the people, if that is the case you can bet against them. Information is very valuable to traders, and this is a new form of collecting and being aware of it. There is little to be gained from pretending this paradigm does not exist and does not pose a risk to your investment. Part of dealing with and controlling the gamification/meme-fication of trading is becoming acquainted with it.

The embrace-the-change camp believes the gamification of finance poses an opportunity and new form of risk management. But a warning should come with this advice: it will be a learning experience. In other words, you should be prepared to lose money and get heartbroken. This is important especially if you are a fresh investor. As a fresh investor you have not built up the critical skills that can insulate you from the worst advice you might encounter or you do not have access to quality information. You are still trying to figure things out for yourself. But as you do and learn, that is where the value of this advice comes. You will become adept at anticipating and monetizing your participation in these spaces.

You can turn a part of your portfolio to exploring that space and honing your skills at sentiment and social media-driven investing. I know as I say these words they are anathema to the more experienced traders and the old guard, but if this is the future, as it appears it might be, we need to start getting the hang of it now. But all this is predicated on the idea that things are moving in this direction, but a lot can happen. Regulation from the state might stem the problem before it gets any worse or step in to make sure that things work a lot more traditionally. But looking at how our governments have struggled to reign in or regulate social media, this might be a beast of its own in much the same way. As I said, while I am going to tell you what they say, it is up to you to make up your mind.

We Are in a Bubble so Don't Bother

There are some worries that what we are seeing now are signs of a bubble. One of the markers of a bubble is that there is general enthusiasm about investing and a lot of people believe, for better or for worse, that they can give good investment advice even when they are not experts themselves. Stories of people becoming millionaires or making thousands from trading are becoming commonplace. That is one of the things that you will notice in times of a bubble as it was in the roaring twenties before the crash. A lot of people look at the market as a way of achieving financial freedom and there is a rise in speculation. And during the pandemic a lot of money went into the markets, potentially inflating prices. This has led some analysts to believe that we are in some sort of a bubble.

That would mean all the activity we see, about millions getting into trading and quitting their jobs, is all because of the bubble, and once it bursts people will wake up and make more sober decisions with their money. The "it's a bubble" crowd has a point, but we cannot pin it on all the activity we have been seeing on that rationale alone. For one, people are much more informed about the markets and finance than they were a hundred years ago. That does not mean we are not susceptible to the same kinds of biases or that the markets haven't become more complex, they have. But what I am pointing to is the fact that despite all of that, people are generally much more informed these days and can learn a lot online through free courses and paid courses about finance and trading. Those people also read books like this one.

Sure, there is a lot of garbage information online about markets, and the way our online spaces are put together can make it hard to find quality information, and there are scams abound, but it wouldn't be entirely accurate to treat what is going on here as a fad. Some of what we see today will stick around even if it dies down in popularity in the future.

Again, I leave it to you to take up your mind about the entire situation.

What Does it Mean for Options Trading?

This is related to options trading because options are one of the most popular financial instruments for new traders on platforms like Robinhood; if it affects stocks and other instruments, it makes sense to pay attention to it and know about it. This is the one chapter in this book that does not try to teach you anything. I am just informing you of something that is worth watching and taking seriously.

The last thing I should add is that it makes sense to take some of the advice in the above sections while also reading about the world of finance from more reputable sources, like Financial Times, Wall Street Journal, Bloomberg, and others. They can be expensive, but you can find some inexpensive way of getting access to that information and letting yourself learn about the financial world outside of the online silos. This will help you form a more balanced view of what is going on and a clear picture of what your outlook should be on any given opportunity and avoid financial landmines.

Chapter 8: Monitoring Your Trades

If you want to learn from your own experience and you truly believe that trading for yourself is valuable skills, this chapter is for you. We'll talk about habits you should implement in your trading to improve your skills. Below are steps you should follow.

Keep Records

Most brokerages will keep a history of all your trades and activity on their platforms. So you will be able to go back and look at it. That information should include when you made a transaction and what was the result. It is more useful when it includes what you believed when you made those decisions. For instance, if you bought a call option, it should have information on whether you were bearish on the underlying stock and the strategy the transaction belonged to.

When your records are this detailed, you can look at yourself as you were, instead of relying on your memory, which is often unreliable and misleading. You should not take the chance especially when it comes to things as important as money. You can use them to gauge your performance and determine your rate of success or your results compared to expectations you had. But even more important is discovering habits and biases that came into play when you made those decisions. You are much more aware of your shortcomings.

If your platform does not offer tools as detailed as these ones, you need to find another solution. For instance, if you cannot record some of your beliefs and expectations within the platform, you can record it in a diary or somewhere easy to find and a match to the history on your platform.

Evaluating Your Trades

Evaluating your trades is all about finding out why some trades were successful and why others weren't. This will help you pinpoint a winning and losing trade before you put it into action. Of course, there will always be extenuating circumstances for each trade because each trade is different.

When evaluating your trades, you need to look at what your losing trades have in common and what your winning trades have in common. For instance, if you found that whenever you used a particular strategy, even if you thought you would lose money, you instead made money, maybe that strategy works for you. That analysis is more reliable the bigger the sample size. For instance, you can't just look at trades made within a month and base all your theories on that information. You should always reevaluate and redefine your theories the more you add data. If those theories and insights still hold and become even stronger with each batch, then they are based on something real.

Optimizing Your Trading

Now that you recognize patterns that are working for you, your biases and shortcomings, you need to use that knowledge to improve your chances. You should repeat the patterns that work for you and avoid the ones that don't. As you do this, you should remember that markets are always changing, and these same methods won't always work. They are only working because they exist in a specific environment, and if that environment changes, those strategies will cease to be effective. Therefore, this process needs to be checked and repeated.

It is necessary to pay attention to general market conditions and be able to tell if they are hospitable to your methods. Paying attention to narratives and mood of the markets is one way of doing this. From there, reevaluate and review your trading plan accordingly. If you recognize any parts of a strategy or approach that need tinkering, then change it.

Last Words

Following these three steps is all you need to ensure that you will always grow, and that process of growing is conscious. You can't just expect that doing something will eventually lead to growth. If you want to be quick at it and continue improving, you need to take conscious steps.

Conclusion

This had been a long, tremendous journey and there was a lot to unpack. We have learned that options are versatile financial instruments that can be used in a variety of ways. They can be used to ride stocks, hedge positions, bet on the outcome of indices, earn extra money from stock you hold, and more. We have learned that options are complex but shouldn't be feared, with a little knowledge, consideration, and practice anyone can be successful trading options. But if I were to boil down the lesson of this book into a few points, they would be these ones:

One: understand your assets. It is important to have a deep understanding of the underlying asset and the conditions that affect it because that will define the behavior of your options. Once you know how your options should behave, you will have a better idea of what looks like a good option and what doesn't. This minimizes the amount of hard work you have to do because options are already complex instruments that take into account extra variables.

Second: be deliberate about your trades. Always think through your trades. Never trade on a whim or hunch. It might work once, but that is pure luck. At the end of the day, luck doesn't quite cut it. You need to think through all aspects of your trade, the strategy you will use, the risk you are taking, and your goals. The more detailed and thorough the better because you can always go back and improve on it.

Three: know the world. This one is much broader, but it pertains to paying attention to trends and issues that may have an impact on the market as a whole. Some of these trends are signs of something deeper, some reveal hidden opportunities, and some show hidden risks that lurk beyond asset-relevant information. Be involved and interact with other traders so you know who you are trading with. A good business knows its customers; other traders are both your customers and competitors, so understand them.

Lastly: keep improving. Always try to improve and hone yourself and be patient while you are doing it. That is the sure way you will see growing returns. It is not all about picking the right socks or strategies. It is also about having perceptiveness. That perceptiveness can only come about through experience and practice. So don't be afraid to learn and grow.

If you have enjoyed this book, please leave a review on Amazon or wherever you found it; it really helps.

References

All images taken from Pexels.

Hayes, A. (2020, May 7). *Bollinger Band®*. Investopedia. https://www.investopedia.com/terms/b/bollingerbands.asp

How to Plan Individual Options Trades. (n.d.). Www.optionstrading.org. https://www.optionstrading.org/getting-started/planning-trades/

Investopedia Team. (2021, January 4). *Types of Options Positions That Create Unlimited Liability*. Investopedia. https://www.investopedia.com/ask/answers/050115/what-types-options-positions-create-unlimited-liability.asp

Johnson, C., & Lewis, J. (2010, September 17). *Options Expiration - What Happens to In-the-Money Puts?* InvestorPlace. https://investorplace.com/2010/09/options-expiration-and-in-the-money-puts/

Milton, A. (2021, June 21). *Learn the Lingo With These Important Options Trading Terms.* The Balance. https://www.thebalance.com/options-strike-price-exercise-price-and-expiration-date-1031126

Monna. (2021, May 1). *Binary options Thailand: What is the best indicator for binary options.* Binary Options Thailand. https://odrivekeu.blogspot.com/2021/05/what-is-best-indicator-for-binary.html

Money Morning Staff. (2019, August 9). How to Make Money Trading Options in 2021. Money Morning - We Make Investing Profitable. https://moneymorning.com/2019/08/09/how-to-make-money-trading-options-in-2020/

Murphy, C. (2021, June 14). *What Is a Put-Call Ratio?* Investopedia. https://www.investopedia.com/ask/answers/06/putcallratio.asp

Peterson, N. (2017, June 5). *Common Pitfalls for New Options Traders.* Schwab Brokerage. https://www.schwab.com/resource-center/insights/content/beginner-options-trading-pitfalls-and-mistakes

Royal, J., & Davis, C. (2021, June 4). *How to Trade Options: First Steps for Beginners.* NerdWallet. https://www.nerdwallet.com/article/investing/how-to-trade-options

Seth, S. (2020). *The Top Technical Indicators for Options Trading.* Investopedia. https://www.investopedia.com/articles/active-trading/101314/top-technical-indicators-options-trading.asp

Sival, S. (2020, October 2). *Risk & Money Management In Option Trading | Replete Equities.* Replete Equities. https://www.repleteequities.com/risk-money-management-in-option-trading-2/

The Options Playbook. (n.d.). 5 Trading Mistakes to Avoid When Trading Options. Www.optionsplaybook.com. Retrieved June 30, 2021, from https://www.optionsplaybook.com/rookies-corner/five-options-trading-mistakes/

Yochim, D. (2016, November 16). *Options Trading Terms and Definitions*. NerdWallet. https://www.nerdwallet.com/article/investing/options-trading-definitions